CHRIST AND THE DRAGON

The Development
of the Conflict Between Christ and Satan
as Revealed in the Books of
Daniel and Revelation

About the Cover
CHRIST
*"He planted his right foot on the sea
and his left foot on the land"*
Rev. 10:2

THE DRAGON
*"And the dragon stood on the shore
of the sea"*
Rev. 13:1

Cover Art
by
Lois Barnes

Maurice Hoppe, Master of Arts
Bible and Systematic Theology
Seventh-day Adventist Theological Seminary

Copyright © 1995 by
Maurice Hoppe

All Rights Reserved

Library of Congress Catalog Card
Number 95-078937

ISBN 0-927022-19-2

Distributed by
Revelation Ministry
P. O. Box 184
Days Creek, Oregon, 97429
(541) 825-3538

Printed by

CHJ Publishing
1103 West Main
Middleton, Idaho 83644

Printed in United States of America

PREFACE

This study guide quotes prophetic chapters of the book of Daniel and text from the book of Revelation in the left column. In the right column the author shares explanatory comments and Biblical references that clarify the text in the left column. The author also shows comparison of similar verses.

All Bible texts are quoted from the New International Version. (Grand Rapids: Zondervan Bible Publishers, 1985)

The large time line chart in the appendix is designed to help the reader understand the relationship of the various prophecies. Hence, it is clearly seen that The Word of God concludes the controversy between Christ and Satan. The student sees how all of the prophecies of the Bible focus on the Second Advent of Jesus when He comes as "King of kings and Lord of lords" to take His faithful people to be with Him forever.

INTRODUCTION

Dear Reader:

The long reign of sin in this world is soon to end. Violence and crime, pleasure-seeking and selfish indulgence, famine and disasters fill the land. Many despair for the future.

But our Father in Heaven, who loves you and me so much that He gave His Son on the cross of Calvary, has provided for us hope for the future.

It is the desire of the author that this study guide on the prophetic books of Daniel and Revelation will help you to find Jesus Christ, the Desire of Ages for your soul.

The Word of God, in the first chapters of Genesis, tells us of our origin by the hand of God. The third chapter reveals the terrible fall of man, but our loving heavenly Father did not leave us in hopeless despair. He gave to Adam and Eve, you and me, that wonderful promise of hope in Genesis 3:15. There was to be a controversy between Christ and Satan over the law of God and this controversy involves every one of us on earth.

"I will put enmity between you and the woman." Enmity means "a bitter feeling of hatred, animosity."

This hatred is to continue between the serpent and his offspring and the woman and her offspring until the time when the earth will again be restored to its original creation.

The outcome of this great struggle between the serpent and the woman is also given in this verse. God said to the serpent "he will crush your head, and you will strike his heel."

In the Bible a pure woman is a symbol of the faithful believers in Christ. It was into this church that Christ came to earth. The serpent struck at His heel when he had Jesus nailed to the cross. But it was through this very act that Christ gained power to strike the head of the serpent.

When the controversy is finished, Christ will cast Satan and his followers into the lake of fire. See Rev 20:10, 14, 15.

It is the objective of this study guide to help you to understand the controversy between the serpent and the woman as God reveals it in the books of Daniel and Revelation. In these books God identifies the forces of this world who are aligned with the serpent and outlines their objectives. God also reveals the identity of the woman and her offspring.

The controversy story draws to a close with the final destruction of the forces of evil and a brief description of the glorious rewards for everyone who overcomes through the Lord Jesus.

You will find yourself in the midst of this controversy. The decisions you make will place you on one side or the other in this great controversy between the woman and her offspring and the serpent (Satan) and his offspring.

My prayer is that you, dear reader, will find your victory in Jesus and in Him find life eternal.

The Lord bless you and keep you;
The Lord make His face shine upon you and be
    gracious to you;
The Lord turn His face toward you and give
    you peace.

Num 6:24–26

TABLE OF CONTENTS

I THE PROPHECIES OF DANIEL

Introduction 1
Nebuchadnezzar's Dream — Dan 2:1-45 2
The Four Beasts and the Little Horn — Dan 7 9
Ram, Goat and Powerful Horn — Dan 8 14
Daniel's Prayer — Dan 9:1-19 19
The Seventy "Sevens" — Dan 9:20-27 22
The Two Sanctuary Services 25
The Time of The End — Dan 12 30

II THE PROPHECIES OF REVELATION

Introduction 32
Prologue — Rev 1:1-3 33

III THE CHARACTERS, PLOT AND SETTING

The Dragon — Rev 12:7-9 34
The Pure Woman — Rev 12:1-5, 10-12 34
The Plot — Rev 12:6, 13-17 36
The Throne in Heaven — Rev 4 37
The Scroll and the Lamb — Rev 5 39

IV SATAN'S KINGDOM

The First Four Seals — Rev 6:1-8 41
The Woman and the Beast — Rev 17:1-15 43
The Beast out of the Sea — Rev 13:1-10 45
The Beast out of the Earth — Rev 13:11-18 47

V CHRIST'S KINGDOM

Christ Introduces Himself — Rev 1:4-20 50
To the Church in Ephesus — Rev 2:1-7 52
To the Church in Smyrna — Rev 2:8-11 53
To the Church in Pergamum — Rev 2:12-17 54
To the Church in Thyatira — Rev 2:18-29 56
To the Church in Sardis — Rev 3:1-6 57
To the Church in Philadelphia — Rev 3:7-13 58
To the Church in Laodicea — Rev 3:14-22 60

VI THE EVERLASTING GOSPEL AND ITS COUNTERFEIT

The Two Witnesses — Rev 11:1-13 62
The Angel and the Scroll — Rev 10 64
Signs Reveal Judgment Time — Rev 6:9-13 66
The Three Angels' Messages 67
    The First Angel 67
        Rev 14:6, 7; 11:19; 19:1-10
    The Second Angel 69
        Rev 14:8; 18:1-8
    The Third Angel 71
        Rev 14:9-13
144,000 Sealed — Rev 7:1-8 72
The Three Evil Spirits — Rev 16:13-16 73
Closing Remarks of God the Father — Rev 21:5-8 . . . 73
Closing Remarks of Jesus — Rev 22:7, 12-16, 20 74
Closing Remarks of The Holy Spirit — Rev 22:17 75
Closing Remarks of John — Rev 22:8-11, 18-21 76

VII THE CONCLUSION OF THE CONTROVERSY

Seven Angels With Seven Plagues 78
    Rev 15:1, 5-8; 16:1
The First Plague — Rev 16:2 79
The Second Plague — Rev 16:3 79
The Third Plague — Rev 16:4-7 80
The Fourth Plague — Rev 16:8, 9 80
The Fifth Plague — Rev 16:10, 11 81
The Sixth Plague 81
    Rev 16:12; 17:1, 2, 16-18; 18:9-24
The Seventh Plague — Rev 16:17-21; 85
    19:11-16; 8:1; 6:14-17; 14:14-20; 19:17-21
The Lamb and the 144,000 — Rev 14:1-5 90
Victorious on the Sea of Glass — Rev 15:2-4. 91
The Great Multitude — Rev 7:9-17. 92
The Thousand Years — Rev 20:1-6 95
Holy City Descends From Heaven — Rev 21:1-4 96
Satan's Kingdom Destroyed — Rev 20:7-15. 97
The New Jerusalem — Rev 21:9-27 98
The River of Life — Rev 22:1-6 101

INDEX OF CHARTS AND DIAGRAMS

Comparison of Visions in Dan 2, 7 and 8 18
The Seventy Sevens (Weeks) 24
The 2,300 Days (Years) 24
Diagram of the Sanctuary 29
Probation to Millennium 94
The Controversy Chronologically Developed . . 102

APPENDIX

General Notes 108
Filth of Her Adulteries 103
The Ten Commandments 105

I THE PROPHECIES OF DANIEL

INTRODUCTION

This part of the study guide will trace the development of the controversy between Christ and Satan as God revealed it in the prophetic chapters of Daniel 2, 7, 8, 9 and 12.

These chapters form the foundation on which the book of Revelation is written and interpreted.

NEBUCHADNEZZAR'S DREAM

Daniel 2:1–45

In the second year of his reign, Nebuchadnezzar had dreams; his mind was troubled and he could not sleep. 2 So the king summoned the magicians, enchanters, sorcerers and astrologers to tell him what he had dreamed. When they came in and stood before the king, 3 he said to them, "I have had a dream that troubles me and I want to know what it means."

4 Then the astrologers answered the king in Aramaic, "O king, live forever! Tell your servants the dream, and we will interpret it."

5 The king replied to the astrologers, "This is what I have firmly decided: If you do not tell me what my dream was and interpret it, I will have you cut into pieces and your houses turned into piles of rubble. 6 But if you tell me the dream and explain it, you will receive from me gifts and rewards and great honor. So tell me the dream and interpret it for me."

7 Once more they replied, "Let the king tell his servants the dream, and we will interpret it."

604 B.C.

Daniel was taken captive in 605 B.C.

He was at this time in the early part of his 3-year training period. Dan 1:5, 6.

The king was unable to remember the subject of his dream, so he required the wise men to tell him his dream and the interpretation.

Daniel 2:1–45 (Cont'd)

8 Then the king answered, "I am certain that you are trying to gain time, because you realize that this is what I have firmly decided: 9 If you do not tell me the dream, there is just one penalty for you. You have conspired to tell me misleading and wicked things, hoping the situation will change. So then, tell me the dream, and I will know that you can interpret it for me."

10 The astrologers answered the king, "There is not a man on earth who can do what the king asks! No king, however great and mighty, has ever asked such a thing of any magician or enchanter or astrologer. 11 What the king asks is too difficult. No one can reveal it to the king except the gods, and they do not live among men."

12 This made the king so angry and furious that he ordered the execution of all the wise men of Babylon. 13 So the decree was issued to put the wise men to death, and men were sent to look for Daniel and his friends to put them to death.

14 When Arioch, the commander of the king's guard,

The astrologers always claimed to be able to communicate with the gods. In their extremity, they acknowledge the fact that this was a false claim.

Daniel 2:1–45 (Cont'd)

had gone out to put to death the wise men of Babylon, Daniel spoke to him with wisdom and tact. 15 He asked the king's officer, "Why did the king issue such a harsh decree?" Arioch then explained the matter to Daniel. 16 At this, Daniel went in to the king and asked for time, so that he might interpret the dream for him.

17 Then Daniel returned to his house and explained the matter to his friends Hananiah, Mishael and Azariah. 18 He urged them to plead for mercy from the God of heaven concerning this mystery, so that he and his friends might not be executed with the rest of the wise men of Babylon. 19 During the night the mystery was revealed to Daniel in a vision. Then Daniel praised the God of heaven 20 and said: "Praise be to the name of God for ever and ever; wisdom and power are his.

21 He changes times and seasons; he sets up kings and deposes them. He gives wisdom to the wise and knowledge to the discerning.

The God of Heaven is a living God and can reveal dreams. This He did for Daniel and gave Daniel the interpretation.

Daniel 2:1–45 (Cont'd)

22 He reveals deep and hidden things; he knows what lies in darkness, and light dwells with him.

23 I thank and praise you, O God of my fathers: You have given me wisdom and power, you have made known to me what we asked of you, you have made known to us the dream of the king."

24 Then Daniel went to Arioch, whom the king had appointed to execute the wise men of Babylon, and said to him, "Do not execute the wise men of Babylon. Take me to the king, and I will interpret his dream for him."

25 Arioch took Daniel to the king at once and said, "I have found a man among the exiles from Judah who can tell the king what his dream means."

26 The king asked Daniel (also called Belteshazzar), "Are you able to tell me what I saw in my dream and interpret it?"

27 Daniel replied, "No wise man, enchanter, magician or diviner can explain to the king the mystery he has asked about,

Daniel 2:1–45 (Cont'd)

28 but there is a God in heaven who reveals mysteries. He has shown King Nebuchadnezzar what will happen in days to come. Your dream and the visions that passed through your mind as you lay on your bed are these:

29 "As you were lying there, O king, your mind turned to things to come, and the revealer of mysteries showed you what is going to happen. 30 As for me, this mystery has been revealed to me, not because I have greater wisdom than other living men, but so that you, O king, may know the interpretation and that you may understand what went through your mind.

31 "You looked, O king, and there before you stood a large statue—an enormous, dazzling statue, awesome in appearance. 32 The head of the statue was made of pure gold, its chest and arms of silver, its belly and thighs of bronze, 33 its legs of iron, its feet partly of iron and partly of baked clay. 34 While you were watching, a rock was cut out, but not by human hands. It struck the statue on its

Daniel pointed Nebuchadnezzar to the God in heaven as the only true God who can reveal dreams and their interpretation.

Daniel reveals the dream.

Daniel 2:1–45 (Cont'd)

feet of iron and clay and smashed them. 35 Then the iron, the clay, the bronze, the silver and the gold were broken to pieces at the same time and became like chaff on a threshing floor in the summer. The wind swept them away without leaving a trace. But the rock that struck the statue became a huge mountain and filled the whole earth.

36 "This was the dream, and now we will interpret it to the king. 37 You, O king, are the king of kings. The God of heaven has given you dominion and power and might and glory; 38 in your hands he has placed mankind and the beasts of the field and the birds of the air. Wherever they live, he has made you ruler over them all. You are that head of gold.

39 "After you, another kingdom will rise, inferior to yours. Next, a third kingdom, one of bronze, will rule over the whole earth. 40 Finally, there will be a fourth kingdom, strong as iron—for iron breaks and smashes everything—and as iron breaks things to pieces, so it will crush and break all the others.

Daniel interprets the dream.

The rulers of the earth are given their power and authority by the God of heaven.

Babylon was represented as the head of gold.

Each metal is a symbol of a political power or nation.
Babylon was overthrown by the kingdom of Medo-Persia. Dan 5:30. Two more kingdoms were to follow in the history of nations.

Daniel 2:1–45 (Cont'd)

41 Just as you saw that the feet and toes were partly of baked clay and partly of iron, so this will be a divided kingdom; yet it will have some of the strength of iron in it, even as you saw iron mixed with clay. 42 As the toes were partly iron and partly clay, so this kingdom will be partly strong and partly brittle. 43 And just as you saw the iron mixed with baked clay, so the people will be a mixture and will not remain united, any more than iron mixes with clay.

44 "In the time of those kings, the God of heaven will set up a kingdom that will never be destroyed, nor will it be left to another people. It will crush all those kingdoms and bring them to an end, but it will itself endure forever. 45 This is the meaning of the vision of the rock cut out of a mountain, but not by human hands—a rock that broke the iron, the bronze, the clay, the silver and the gold to pieces.

"The great God has shown the king what will take place in the future. The dream is true and the interpretation is trustworthy."

This indicates that a group of independent political nations would come into existence following the fourth world power.

In the end the God of Heaven will destroy all the nations of this world and set up His own Kingdom which will last forever.

A rock — Trust in the Lord forever, for the Lord, the Lord is the Rock eternal. Isa 26:4

THE FOUR BEASTS AND THE LITTLE HORN

Daniel 7

In the first year of Belshazzar king of Babylon, Daniel had a dream, and visions passed through his mind as he was lying on his bed. He wrote down the substance of his dream.

2 Daniel said: "In my vision at night I looked, and there before me were the four winds of heaven churning up the great sea. 3 Four great beasts, each different from the others, came up out of the sea.

4 "The first was like a lion, and it had the wings of an eagle. I watched until its wings were torn off and it was lifted from the ground so that it stood on two feet like a man, and the heart of a man was given to it.

5 "And there before me was a second beast, which looked like a bear. It was raised up on one of its sides, and it had three ribs in its mouth between its teeth. It was told, 'Get up and eat your fill of flesh!'

6 "After that, I looked, and there before me was another beast, one that looked like a

553 B.C. or 50 years following the dream of Nebuchadnezzar in Daniel 2. This time the dream was given to Daniel.

Beasts are symbols of nations. Dan 7:17

Comparison of Dan 2 with Dan 7

Lion
Head of gold   Dan 2:32
* Babylon   Dan 2:38*
626 B.C. to 539 B.C.

Bear
Chest and arms of silver
* Dan 2:32, 39*
* Medo-Persia   Dan 5:30*
539 B.C. to 330 B.C.

Daniel 7 (Cont'd)

leopard. And on its back it had four wings like those of a bird. This beast had four heads, and it was given authority to rule.

7 "After that, in my vision at night I looked, and there before me was a fourth beast—terrifying and frightening and very powerful. It had large iron teeth; it crushed and devoured its victims and trampled underfoot whatever was left. It was different from all the former beasts, and it had ten horns.

8 "While I was thinking about the horns, there before me was another horn, a little one, which came up among them; and three of the first horns were uprooted before it. This horn had eyes like the eyes of a man and a mouth that spoke boastfully.

9 "As I looked, thrones were set in place, and the Ancient of Days took his seat. His clothing was as white as snow; the hair of his head was white like wool. His throne was flaming with fire, and its wheels were all ablaze.

10 A river of fire was flowing, coming out from before him. Thousands upon thousands attended him; ten thousand times

Leopard
Belly and thighs of bronze
  Dan 2:32, 39
  Greece followed Medo-Persia. Dan 8:20, 21
  330 B.C. to its gradual demise ending during the first century B.C.

Fourth beast
Legs of iron Dan 2:33, 40
  Large iron teeth
  Rome followed Greece in the history of nations.

Ten Horns
Feet and toes of iron and clay
  Dan 2:33, 40-43
Horns are symbolic of kings or nations. Dan 7:24; Rev 17:12

Historically the ten divisions of the Roman empire were:
  1 Huns   6 Suevi
  2 Ostrogoths 7 Burgundians
  3 Visigoths   8 Heruli
  4 Franks   9 Anglo-Saxons
  5 Vandals   10 Lombards
The three powers uprooted were:
  1 Heruli   493 A.D.
  2 Vandals   534 A.D.
  3 Ostrogoths   538-553 A.D.

Daniel 7 (Cont'd)

ten thousand stood before him. The court was seated, and the books were opened.

11 "Then I continued to watch because of the boastful words the horn was speaking. I kept looking until the beast was slain and its body destroyed and thrown into the blazing fire. 12 (The other beasts had been stripped of their authority, but were allowed to live for a period of time.)

13 "In my vision at night I looked, and there before me was one like a son of man, coming with the clouds of heaven. He approached the Ancient of Days and was led into his presence. 14 He was given authority, glory and sovereign power; all peoples, nations and men of every language worshiped him. His dominion is an everlasting dominion that will not pass away, and his kingdom is one that will never be destroyed.

15 "I, Daniel, was troubled in spirit, and the visions that passed through my mind disturbed me. 16 I approached one of those standing there and asked him the true meaning of all this.

"So he told me and gave me the interpretation of these things:

Judgment scene

One like a son of man — Jesus Christ — Matt 8:20 Compare Rev 14:14

Compare Dan 2:44, 45

Notice that the broad outline presented here is similar to that represented by the image of Daniel 2.

Daniel 7 (Cont'd)

17 'The four great beasts are four kingdoms that will rise from the earth. 18 But the saints of the Most High will receive the kingdom and will possess it forever—yes, for ever and ever.'

19 "Then I wanted to know the true meaning of the fourth beast, which was different from all the others and most terrifying, with its iron teeth and bronze claws—the beast that crushed and devoured its victims and trampled underfoot whatever was left. 20 I also wanted to know about the ten horns on its head and about the other horn that came up, before which three of them fell—the horn that looked more imposing than the others and that had eyes and a mouth that spoke boastfully. 21 As I watched, this horn was waging war against the saints and defeating them, 22 until the Ancient of Days came and pronounced judgment in favor of the saints of the Most High, and the time came when they possessed the kingdom.

23 "He gave me this explanation: 'The fourth beast is a fourth kingdom that will appear on earth. It will be

Both dreams depict four world kingdoms.

Both conclude with the God of heaven establishing His Kingdom on earth forever.

Compare Dan 2:40

Daniel 7 (Cont'd)

different from all the other kingdoms and will devour the whole earth, trampling it down and crushing it. 24 The ten horns are ten kings who will come from this kingdom. After them another king will arise, different from the earlier ones; he will subdue three kings. 25 He will speak against the Most High and oppress his saints and try to change the set times and the laws. The saints will be handed over to him for a time, times and half a time.

26 " 'But the court will sit, and his power will be taken away and completely destroyed forever. 27 Then the sovereignty, power and greatness of the kingdoms under the whole heaven will be handed over to the saints, the people of the Most High. His kingdom will be an everlasting kingdom, and all rulers will worship and obey him.'

28 "This is the end of the matter. I, Daniel, was deeply troubled by my thoughts, and my face turned pale, but I kept the matter to myself."

Compare Dan 7:8

In prophecy:

Time   = 1 yr. = 360 days
Times   = 2 yrs. = 720 days
½ Time = ½ yr. = 180 days
*   1,260 days*

We are not told here where this period of time fits into prophecy. Court will sit — Dan 7: 9, 10, 13

Compare Dan 2:44, 45
Daniel 7 gives significantly more detail of the controversy between the powers on earth and the God of heaven. God now begins to unveil the conflict between the serpent and his followers and the woman and her seed. See Gen 3:15. The God of heaven gave this information for all who live on earth to understand.

RAM, GOAT AND POWERFUL HORN

Daniel 8

In the third year of King Belshazzar's reign, I, Daniel, had a vision, after the one that had already appeared to me. 2 In my vision I saw myself in the citadel of Susa in the province of Elam; in the vision I was beside the Ulai Canal. 3 I looked up, and there before me was a ram with two horns, standing beside the canal, and the horns were long. One of the horns was longer than the other but grew up later. 4 I watched the ram as he charged toward the west and the north and the south. No animal could stand against him, and none could rescue from his power. He did as he pleased and became great.

5 As I was thinking about this, suddenly a goat with a prominent horn between his eyes came from the west, crossing the whole earth without touching the ground. 6 He came toward the two-horned ram I had seen standing beside the canal and charged at him in great rage.

551 B.C. Two years following the vision of Daniel 7

Daniel 8 (Cont'd)

7 I saw him attack the ram furiously, striking the ram and shattering his two horns. The ram was powerless to stand against him; the goat knocked him to the ground and trampled on him, and none could rescue the ram from his power. 8 The goat became very great, but at the height of his power his large horn was broken off, and in its place four prominent horns grew up toward the four winds of heaven.

9 Out of one of them came another horn, which started small but grew in power to the south and to the east and toward the Beautiful Land. 10 It grew until it reached the host of the heavens, and it threw some of the starry host down to the earth and trampled on them. 11 It set itself up to be as great as the Prince of the host; it took away the daily sacrifice from him, and the place of his sanctuary was brought low. 12 Because of rebellion, the host of the saints and the daily sacrifice were given over to it. It prospered in everything it did, and truth was thrown to the ground.

Daniel 8 (Cont'd)

13 Then I heard a holy one speaking, and another holy one said to him, "How long will it take for the vision to be fulfilled—the vision concerning the daily sacrifice, the rebellion that causes desolation, and the surrender of the sanctuary and of the host that will be trampled underfoot?"

14 He said to me, "It will take 2,300 evenings and mornings; then the sanctuary will be reconsecrated."

15 While I, Daniel, was watching the vision and trying to understand it, there before me stood one who looked like a man. 16 And I heard a man's voice from the Ulai calling, "Gabriel, tell this man the meaning of the vision."

17 As he came near the place where I was standing, I was terrified and fell prostrate. "Son of man," he said to me, "understand that the vision concerns the time of the end."

18 While he was speaking to me, I was in a deep sleep, with my face to the ground. Then he touched me and raised me to my feet.

For explanation of this text, see Dan 9:24-27, the 2,300-year diagram on p. 24 and the discussion of the two sanctuaries beginning on p. 25.

Daniel 8 (Cont'd)

19 He said: "I am going to tell you what will happen later in the time of wrath, because the vision concerns the appointed time of the end. 20 The two-horned ram that you saw represents the kings of Media and Persia. 21 The shaggy goat is the king of Greece, and the large horn between his eyes is the first king. 22 The four horns that replaced the one that was broken off represent four kingdoms that will emerge from his nation but will not have the same power.

23 "In the latter part of their reign, when rebels have become completely wicked, a stern-faced king, a master of intrigue, will arise. 24 He will become very strong, but not by his own power. He will cause astounding devastation and will succeed in whatever he does. He will destroy the mighty men and the holy people. 25 He will cause deceit to prosper, and he will consider himself superior. When they feel secure, he will destroy many and take his stand against the Prince of princes. Yet he will be destroyed, but not by human power.

God begins to focus our attention on the "time of the end." He does not tell us here where the "time of the end" fits into prophecy. We now see that this vision also is parallel to the visions of Daniel 2 and 7. Babylon is not mentioned here.

Two-horned ram — Medo-Persia
  Chest and arms of silver
  The bear
Shaggy goat — Greece
  Belly and thighs of bronze
  Leopard
Large horn — Alexander the
  Great — Dan 8:8
Four horns
  Four generals who divided Greece following Alexander's death
  Cassander   — Area of Greece
  Lysimachus — Area of Asia Minor
  Seleucus   — Syria and Babylon
  Ptolemy   — Egypt
Stern-faced king
  Compare Dan 8:9-12, 23-25 with Dan 7:8, 20-25
Compare Dan 8:25 (last part) with Dan 2:44, 45; 7:22, 26, 27

Daniel 8 (Cont'd)

26 "The vision of the evenings and mornings that has been given you is true, but seal up the vision, for it concerns the distant future."

27 I, Daniel, was exhausted and lay ill for several days. Then I got up and went about the king's business. I was appalled by the vision; it was beyond understanding.

The vision of evenings and mornings has reference to Dan 8:14.
Distant future — Compare Dan 8:26 (last part) with Dan 8:19 (last part).

GRAPHIC COMPARISON OF VISIONS OF DANIEL 2, 7 and 8

Daniel 2	Daniel 7	Daniel 8	Text	Nation
Head of gold	Lion	—	Dan 2:38	Babylon 626 BC
Chest and arms of silver	Bear	Ram	Dan 8:20 Dan 5:30, 31	Medo-Persia 539 BC
Belly and thighs of bronze	Leopard	Goat	Dan 8:21	Greece 330 BC
Legs of iron	Terrifying and frightening beast	Another horn; Stern-faced king	History records that Rome followed Greece	Rome gradually came into power in the second and first centuries BC

DANIEL'S PRAYER

Daniel 9:1-19

In the first year of Darius son of Xerxes (a Mede by descent), who was made ruler over the Babylonian kingdom — 2 in the first year of his reign, I, Daniel, understood from the Scriptures, according to the word of the Lord given to Jeremiah the prophet, that the desolation of Jerusalem would last seventy years. 3 So I turned to the Lord God and pleaded with him in prayer and petition, in fasting, and in sackcloth and ashes.

4 I prayed to the Lord my God and confessed: "O Lord, the great and awesome God, who keeps his covenant of love with all who love him and obey his commands, 5 we have sinned and done wrong. We have been wicked and have rebelled; we have turned away from your commands and laws. 6 We have not listened to your servants the prophets, who spoke in your name to our kings, our princes and our fathers, and to all the people of the land.

7 "Lord, you are righteous, but this day we are covered with shame—the men of Judah and

539/538 B.C.
Babylon was captured by Darius the Mede in 539 B.C. Dan 5:30, 31

Jer 25:11, 12
Daniel, taken captive in 605 B.C., hoped to be released soon.

Daniel could not understand the relationship among the 70-year time period prophesied by Jeremiah, the 2,300-day time period in Dan 8:14 and the 1,260-day time period in Dan 7:25. He now turns to God in prayer for light on this subject.

Daniel is concerned about the sins of the people.

Everyone who sins breaks the law; sin is lawlessness. 1 Jn 3:4
Jesus said, "If you love Me, you will obey what I command". Jn 14:15

...1-19 (Cont'd)

people of Jerusalem and all Israel, both near and far, in all the countries where you have scattered us because of our unfaithfulness to you. 8 O Lord, we and our kings, our princes and our fathers are covered with shame because we have sinned against you. 9 The Lord our God is merciful and forgiving, even though we have rebelled against him; 10 we have not obeyed the Lord our God or kept the laws he gave us through his servants the prophets. 11 All Israel has transgressed your law and turned away, refusing to obey you.

"Therefore the curses and sworn judgments written in the Law of Moses, the servant of God, have been poured out on us, because we have sinned against you. 12 You have fulfilled the words spoken against us and against our rulers by bringing upon us great disaster. Under the whole heaven nothing has ever been done like what has been done to Jerusalem. 13 Just as it is written in the Law of Moses, all this disaster has come upon us, yet we have not sought the favor of the Lord our God by turning from our sins and giving attention

See Duet 11:26-28; 27; 28

Daniel 9:1-19 (Cont'd)

to your truth. 14 The lord did not hesitate to bring the disaster upon us, for the Lord our God is righteous in everything he does; yet we have not obeyed him.

15 "Now, O Lord our God, who brought your people out of Egypt with a mighty hand and who made for yourself a name that endures to this day, we have sinned, we have done wrong. 16 O Lord, in keeping with all your righteous acts, turn away your anger and your wrath from Jerusalem, your city, your holy hill. Our sins and the iniquities of our fathers have made Jerusalem and your people an object of scorn to all those around us.

17 "Now, our God, hear the prayers and petitions of your servant. For your sake, O Lord, look with favor on your desolate sanctuary. 18 Give ear, O God, and hear; open your eyes and see the desolation of the city that bears your Name. We do not make requests of you because we are righteous, but because of your great mercy. 19 O Lord, listen! O Lord, forgive! O Lord, hear and act! For your sake, O my God, do not delay, because your city and your people bear your Name."

THE SEVENTY "SEVENS"

Daniel 9:20-27

20 While I was speaking and praying, confessing my sin and the sin of my people Israel and making my request to the Lord my God for his holy hill—21 while I was still in prayer, Gabriel, the man I had seen in the earlier vision, came to me in swift flight about the time of the evening sacrifice. 22 He instructed me and said to me, "Daniel, I have now come to give you insight and understanding. 23 As soon as you began to pray, an answer was given, which I have come to tell you, for you are highly esteemed. Therefore, consider the message and understand the vision:

24 "Seventy 'sevens' are decreed for your people and your holy city to finish transgression, to put an end to sin, to atone for wickedness, to bring in everlasting righteousness, to seal up vision and prophecy and to anoint the most holy.

25 "Know and understand this: From the issuing of the decree to restore and rebuild

Gabriel — Dan 8:16

Give you understanding of the vision in Dan 8:15, 27

70 weeks — part of the 2,300 days (years) of Dan 8:14

Death, burial and resurrection of Jesus

Jesus anointed the Most Holy with His own blood

Decree issued by Artaxerxes in 457 B.C. Ezra 7:12-26

Daniel 9:20–27 (Cont'd)

Jerusalem until the Anointed One, the ruler, comes, there will be seven 'sevens,' and sixty-two 'sevens.' It will be rebuilt with streets and a trench, but in times of trouble. 26 After the sixty-two 'sevens,' the Anointed One will be cut off and will have nothing. The people of the ruler who will come will destroy the city and the sanctuary. The end will come like a flood: War will continue until the end, and desolations have been decreed. 27 He will confirm a covenant with many for one 'seven.' In the middle of the 'seven' he will put an end to sacrifice and offering. And on a wing of the temple he will set up an abomination that causes desolation, until the end that is decreed is poured out on him."

Jesus Christ is the Anointed One. Acts 10:37, 38; Luke 3:21, 22
1 day = 1 year in prophetic time.
Num 14:34; Ezek 4:6

7 "7's"	=	49 days (years)
62 "7's"	=	434 days (years)
69 "7's"	=	483 days (years)

One "7" = 7 days (years)
In the middle of seven years Jesus was crucified. This ended the sacrificial system in 31 A.D. Jesus was baptized in 27 A.D. Stephen was stoned in 34 A.D. Then the gospel went to the Gentiles.

Seventy Sevens (Weeks) Diagram
Daniel 9:24

70 x 7 = 490 days (years)

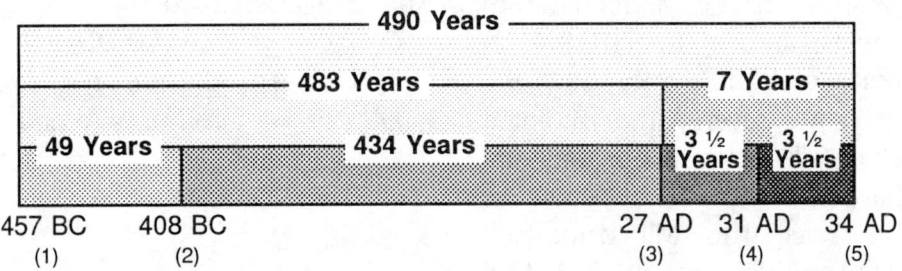

History confirms the interpretation and dates of this time prophecy. Using the day for a year principle, the 490-day prophecy, being a part of the 2,300-day prophecy of Daniel 8:14, establishes 457 BC as the beginning date for the 2,300-day prophecy. The ending date is then 1844 AD.

(1) Command to restore and rebuild Jerusalem Ezra 7:12-28
(2) City and temple rebuilt — Possible reference to Neh 12:27-43
(3) Baptism and anointing of Jesus — Mt 3:13-17; Mk 1:9-11; Lk 3:21, 22; Jn 1:29-34
(4) Jesus crucified — Mt 27:32-54; Mk 15:21-39; Lk 23:26-47; Jn 19:17-37
(5) Stephen stoned — Acts 7:54-60
Gospel goes to Gentiles — Acts 8:4-40

2,300 Days (Years) Diagram
Daniel 8:14

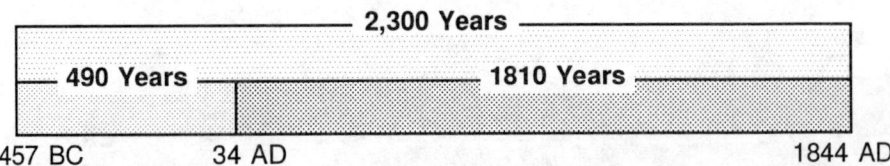

The meaning of the 2,300 day (year) time period was not given to Daniel. His book was shut up and sealed until the time of the end. Dan. 12:9.

THE TWO SANCTUARY SERVICES

Introduction

At this point, we will leave the study of the prophecies of Daniel to briefly discuss the two sanctuaries presented in the Bible. It is not possible to understand the importance and significance of Daniel 8:14 until we have a clear concept of these sanctuaries. The sanctuary on earth is presented in the Old Testament. Its counterpart in heaven is referenced in both the Old and New Testaments.

Daniel 8:14 brings two subjects to our attention:

1) The 2,300 days
2) The cleansing of a sanctuary

The 2,300 days has been presented above. We shall now take up the subject of the "cleansing of the sanctuary." The left column gives a summary of the earthly sanctuary, and the services connected with it. The right column lists Bible references giving detailed information to support these comments.

When the Israelite people were camped at the foot of Mt. Sinai, Moses was instructed to build a sanctuary that God might dwell among them. Instructions were given for the size and construction of the courtyard around the sanctuary.	See Ex 25:8, 9 See Ex 27:9-19; 38:9-20
Very detailed information is given for the construction of the tabernacle itself. The approximate size was 15' by 45'.	See Ex 26:1-37; 36:8-38
Two items for the service of the sanctuary were located in front of the tabernacle in the courtyard. They were the: 1) Altar of burnt offering 2) Laver	 See Ex 27:1-8; 38:1-7 See Ex 30: 17-21; 38:8

The Two Sanctuary Services (Cont'd)

The offerings and animal sacrifices were burned on the altar. The basin contained water for washing and cleansing.

The articles of furniture used in the Holy Place, or the first room as one would enter the sanctuary, were as follows:

   1) Table for the bread — This represented Jesus, the bread of life

See Ex 25:23-30; 37:10-16
See Jn 6:32-51

   2) Lamp stand — This represented Jesus the light of the world

See Ex 25:31-40; 37:17-24
See Jn 8:12; 9:5; 12:46

   3) Altar of incense — This was a symbol of the prayers of the saints ascending to God

See Ex 30:1-10; 37:25-29
See Rev 8:3; 5:8

There was only one article of furniture located in the Most Holy Place, or second room, in the sanctuary. It was the Ark of the Testimony.

See Ex 25:10-22; 37:1-9

The ark contained tables of stone on which were written, by the finger of God, the ten commandments.

See Ex 31:18; 34:1; Heb 9:3, 4
See Heb 9:5

Over the ark were two cherubim and the mercy seat. Over the mercy seat was the Shekinah, the light of God's presence with the people.

The basic service of the sanctuary was the offering of two lambs each day of the year, one in the morning and one in the evening. These lambs were a symbol of Jesus, the Lamb of God, who would give his life to take away the sin of the world.

See Ex 29:38-42

See John 1:29-34

The Two Sanctuary Services (Cont'd)

In type, the sins of the people, which were confessed over the head of the lamb, were transferred to the sanctuary.

Once a year, on the Day of Atonement, the sanctuary was cleansed. That is, the sins that in type collected in the sanctuary were removed.

See Lev 16:2-34; 23:26-32; Num 29:7-11

This was done symbolically with the use of two goats. The Lord's goat was slain and the blood was sprinkled on the mercy seat in the Most Holy Place to make atonement for the sins of the people.

When the High Priest came out from the Most Holy Place, he confessed all the sins over the head of the scapegoat. The scapegoat was then sent to the wilderness, thus symbolizing the removal of sin from the sanctuary, so it was now clean.

This service in the sanctuary on earth was performed in a tent (which was constructed according to the plans that God gave to Moses) from 1443 to 959 B.C., a period of about 485 years.

In 959 B.C. the services were transferred to the temple built by King Solomon. This temple was destroyed by Nebuchadnezzar, king of Babylon, in 586 B.C. Thus, Solomon's temple had a life span of 373 years.

From 586 B.C. to 520 B.C. the temple was in ruins. In 516 B.C. a new temple, built by Zerubbabel, Joshua, Haggai and Zechariah, was dedicated and services were reestablished.

This was the sanctuary that was in use during Jesus' ministry on earth. The veil

The Two Sanctuary Services (Cont'd)

was torn from top to bottom when Jesus died on the cross, thus indicating the end of the sacrificial services.   *See Mt 27:50, 51*

The Jews, however, not accepting Jesus as the Lamb of God, continued sacrificing animals in the temple until it was destroyed in 70 A.D. by the Romans. There has not been a sanctuary for these services on earth since then.

We shall now go back to Exodus 25:8, 9. Here we are told that the sanctuary that God instructed Moses to build was a pattern of another sanctuary. Other verses speak of this sanctuary as a pattern or copy also. Paul says that it was a copy of the sanctuary in heaven.   *See Ex 25:40; 26:30; Num 8:4; Acts 7:44; Heb 8:5*

Now let us return to our text in Daniel 8:14. Daniel said the sanctuary would be cleansed in 2,300 days (years). We found that the 2,300 years terminated in 1844 A.D., therefore it could have no meaning for the sanctuary on earth that has not been in existence since 70 A.D.

In the book of Hebrews, the apostle Paul talks about the sanctuary on earth and the one in heaven. He emphasizes the ministry of Jesus as our High Priest in the Heavenly Sanctuary.   *See Heb 8:1-6; 9:11, 12, 23-28*

The apostle John in Revelation opens to our understanding the sanctuary in heaven. He depicts Jesus as the Lamb, slain on Calvary, appearing before the throne.   *See Rev 5:6*

We shall next consider a few verses in Daniel 12. Then we will turn our attention to the book of Revelation.

Diagram of the Sanctuary

Additional information on pages 108, 109, 110, 111 and 112

THE TIME OF THE END

Daniel 12

"At that time Michael, the great prince who protects your people, will arise. There will be a time of distress such as has not happened from the beginning of nations until then. But at that time your people—everyone whose name is found written in the book—will be delivered. 2 Multitudes who sleep in the dust of the earth will awake: some to everlasting life, others to shame and everlasting contempt. 3 Those who are wise will shine like the brightness of the heavens, and those who lead many to righteousness, like the stars for ever and ever. 4 But you, Daniel, close up and seal the words of the scroll until the time of the end. Many will go here and there to increase knowledge."

5 Then I, Daniel, looked, and there before me stood two others, one on this bank of the river and one on the opposite bank. 6 One of them said to the man clothed in linen, who was above the waters of the river, "How long will it be before these astonishing things are fulfilled?"

Resurrection of the saints
Resurrection of the wicked

The Book of Daniel is not to be understood until the time of the end.

A sign of the time of the end

Or, "When will the time of the end be?"

Daniel 12 (Cont'd)

7 The man clothed in linen, who was above the waters of the river, lifted his right hand and his left hand toward heaven, and I heard him swear by him who lives forever, saying, "It will be for a time, times and half a time. When the power of the holy people has been finally broken, all these things will be completed."

*Time given for "time of the end"
See note on Dan 7:25*

8 I heard, but I did not understand. So I asked, "My lord, what will the outcome of all this be?"

9 He replied, "Go your way, Daniel, because the words are closed up and sealed until the time of the end. 10 Many will be purified, made spotless and refined, but the wicked will continue to be wicked. None of the wicked will understand, but those who are wise will understand.

Compare Dan 12:4

Compare Dan 12:2

11 "From the time that the daily sacrifice is abolished and the abomination that causes desolation is set up, there will be 1,290 days. 12 Blessed is the one who waits for and reaches the end of the 1,335 days.

13 "As for you, go your way till the end. You will rest, and then at the end of the days you will rise to receive your allotted inheritance."

The Lord promises Daniel that he will be raised in the resurrection of the saints. See Dan 12:2

II THE PROPHECIES OF REVELATION

INTRODUCTION

We found in the prophecies of Daniel a brief introduction to a mighty conflict between the nations of this earth and the God of heaven. The saints, believers in the God of creation, are directly affected by this controversy.

Time periods of 1,260 days and 2,300 days were introduced but not explained. The cleansing of the heavenly sanctuary was also not explained.

The book of Revelation is a companion book to Daniel. It is in Revelation that answers are provided for the time prophecies and the cleansing of the sanctuary mentioned in Daniel 8:14.

The reader of Revelation quickly notices that the book is not written in any order or sequence of developing events. Consequently few people read or understand the themes of this book.

The writer of this study guide has organized the chapters and verses of Revelation into themes that develop as if one were reading a story. The characters of the story are introduced first, and the plot is explained. The positions of both sides of the controversy are developed. The climax is reached and the story is brought to a conclusion.

With this approach in mind, after the prologue, we shall begin with Revelation 12:7.

PROLOGUE

Revelation 1:1-3

The revelation of Jesus Christ, which God gave him to show his servants what must soon take place. He made it known by sending his angel to his servant John, 2 who testifies to everything he saw—that is, the word of God and the testimony of Jesus Christ. 3 Blessed is the one who reads the words of this prophecy, and blessed are those who hear it and take to heart what is written in it, because the time is near.

The testimony of Jesus is the spirit of prophecy. Rev 19:10
You receive the blessing of God when you read, hear and obey the words of the Book of Revelation.
The time is near. Dan 12:9

III THE CHARACTERS, PLOT AND SETTING

THE DRAGON

Revelation 12:7-9

7 And there was war in heaven. Michael and his angels fought against the dragon, and the dragon and his angels fought back. 8 But he was not strong enough, and they lost their place in heaven. 9 The great dragon was hurled down—that ancient serpent called the devil, or Satan, who leads the whole world astray. He was hurled to the earth, and his angels with him.

Michael — Christ

The dragon — Satan

Serpent — Gen 3:15; Isa 14:12-15; Eze 28:12-17

THE PURE WOMAN

Revelation 12:1-5, 10-12

A great and wondrous sign appeared in heaven: a woman clothed with the sun, with the moon under her feet and a crown of twelve stars on her head. 2 She was pregnant and cried out in pain as she was about to give birth. 3 Then another sign appeared in heaven:

Woman — Gen 3:15
Clothed with the sun — Symbol of a pure church — her offspring are the saints

Revelation 12:1-5, 10-12 (Cont'd)

an enormous red dragon with seven heads and ten horns and seven crowns on his heads. 4 His tail swept a third of the stars out of the sky and flung them to the earth. The dragon stood in front of the woman who was about to give birth, so that he might devour her child the moment it was born. 5 She gave birth to a son, a male child, who will rule all the nations with an iron scepter. And her child was snatched up to God and to his throne.

10 Then I heard a loud voice in heaven say: "Now have come the salvation and the power and the kingdom of our God, and the authority of his Christ. For the accuser of our brothers, who accuses them before our God day and night, has been hurled down.

11 "They overcame him by the blood of the Lamb and by the word of their testimony; they did not love their lives so much as to shrink from death. 12 Therefore rejoice, you heavens and you who dwell in them! But woe to the earth and the sea, because the devil has gone down to you! He is filled with fury, because he knows that his time is short."

Dragon — Rev 12:4, 7, 9, 13, 16, 17

Tail swept stars to earth — Rev 12:9

Devour her child — Matt 2:16

Birth to a son — Luke 2:1-21; Matt 1:18-25
Rule with an iron scepter — Ps 2:9
Christ snatched up to God — Acts 1:9-11
To His throne — Rev 4; 5:6
Now have come salvation — 2 Cor 5:15, 19; Rom 3:26

The accuser of our brothers — Job 1:9-11; Zech 3:1; 1 Pet 5:8

Blood of the Lamb — 1 Pet 1:18, 19; Eph 1:7

THE PLOT

Revelation 12:6, 13-17

6 The woman fled into the desert to a place prepared for her by God, where she might be taken care of for 1,260 days.

13 When the dragon saw that he had been hurled to the earth, he pursued the woman who had given birth to the male child. 14 The woman was given the two wings of a great eagle, so that she might fly to the place prepared for her in the desert, where she would be taken care of for a time, times and half a time, out of the serpent's reach. 15 Then from his mouth the serpent spewed water like a river, to overtake the woman and sweep her away with the torrent. 16 But the earth helped the woman by opening its mouth and swallowing the river that the dragon had spewed out of his mouth. 17 Then the dragon was enraged at the woman and went off to make war against the rest of her offspring—those who obey God's commandments and hold to the testimony of Jesus.

Woman — Rev 12:1

1,260 days — Rev 12:14; Dan 7:25; 12:7
This places the 1,260 day time period after the birth of Jesus

1,260 days — see note on Dan 7:25

Dragon went to make war — Dan 2:40; 7:19-25; 8:9-12, 23-25
Commandments — Ex 20:3-17
Testimony of Jesus — Rev 19:10

THE THRONE IN HEAVEN

Revelation 4

After this I looked, and there before me was a door standing open in heaven. And the voice I had first heard speaking to me like a trumpet said, "Come up here, and I will show you what must take place after this." 2 At once I was in the Spirit, and there before me was a throne in heaven with someone sitting on it. 3 And the one who sat there had the appearance of jasper and carnelian. A rainbow, resembling an emerald, encircled the throne. 4 Surrounding the throne were twenty-four other thrones, and seated on them were twenty-four elders. They were dressed in white and had crowns of gold on their heads. 5 From the throne came flashes of lightning, rumblings and peals of thunder. Before the throne, seven lamps were blazing. These are the seven spirits of God. 6 Also before the throne there was what looked like a sea of glass, clear as crystal.

In Rev 12:5 we learned that Jesus was taken up to heaven.

In Rev 5:6 we see Jesus, the Lamb, standing in the throne. The setting for this scene begins with Revelation 4.
John is taken by the Holy Spirit to the throne room in heaven and shown what will take place in the future.

A description of God the Father on His throne. Jesus, The Lamb, is seen later standing in the center of the throne. Rev 5:6

Seven lamps — Ex 40:24 — The lampstand was located in the Holy place of the sanctuary on earth.
Jesus entered the Holy Place of the sanctuary in heaven when He was snatched up to God and to His throne. Rev 12:5. This is the beginning of Jesus' ministry in the sanctuary in heaven.
Seven spirits — Isa 11:2 A reference to the Holy Spirit

Revelation 4 (Cont'd)

In the center, around the throne, were four living creatures, and they were covered with eyes, in front and in back. 7 The first living creature was like a lion, the second was like an ox, the third had a face like a man, the fourth was like a flying eagle. 8 Each of the four living creatures had six wings and was covered with eyes all around, even under his wings. Day and night they never stop saying: "Holy, holy, holy is the Lord God Almighty, who was, and is, and is to come." 9 Whenever the living creatures give glory, honor and thanks to him who sits on the throne and who lives for ever and ever, 10 the twenty-four elders fall down before him who sits on the throne, and worship him who lives for ever and ever. They lay their crowns before the throne and say:

11 "You are worthy, our Lord and God, to receive glory and honor and power, for you created all things, and by your will they were created and have their being."

*Four living creatures —
Rev 6:1, 3, 5-7; 15:5-7*

All heaven delights in the worship of the Father

See The Desire of Ages, pp 832-835 for another description of the scene as recorded in Rev 4 and 5.
See Appendix., p. 102.

THE SCROLL AND THE LAMB

Revelation 5

Then I saw in the right hand of him who sat on the throne a scroll with writing on both sides and sealed with seven seals. 2 And I saw a mighty angel proclaiming in a loud voice, "Who is worthy to break the seals and open the scroll?" 3 But no one in heaven or on earth or under the earth could open the scroll or even look inside it. 4 I wept and wept because no one was found who was worthy to open the scroll or look inside. 5 Then one of the elders said to me, "Do not weep! See, the Lion of the tribe of Judah, the Root of David, has triumphed. He is able to open the scroll and its seven seals."

6 Then I saw a Lamb, looking as if it had been slain, standing in the center of the throne, encircled by the four living creatures and the elders. He had seven horns and seven eyes, which are the seven spirits of God sent out into all the earth. 7 He came and took the scroll from the right hand of him who sat on the throne. 8 And when he had taken it, the four living creatures and the twenty-four elders fell down before the Lamb. Each one had a harp

Rev 5 is a continuation of Rev 4. The fact that the scroll is in the hand of God the Father is an indication of the importance of the message it contains.

John was greatly concerned that no one was worthy to open the scroll. This is a second indication of the importance of the message it contains.

Lion of Judah — Gen 49:9, 10
Root of David — Isa 11:1, 10

A Lamb — Symbol of Christ the Lamb of God — Jn 1:29

Seven spirits — Rev 4:5

Revelation 5 (Cont'd)

and they were holding golden bowls full of incense, which are the prayers of the saints. 9 And they sang a new song:

'You are worthy to take the scroll and to open its seals, because you were slain, and with your blood you purchased men for God from every tribe and language and people and nation. 10 "You have made them to be a kingdom and priests to serve our God, and they will reign on the earth."

11 Then I looked and heard the voice of many angels, numbering thousands upon thousands, and ten thousand times ten thousand. They encircled the throne and the living creatures and the elders. 12 In a loud voice they sang: "Worthy is the Lamb, who was slain, to receive power and wealth and wisdom and strength and honor and glory and praise!"

13 Then I heard every creature in heaven and on earth and under the earth and on the sea, and all that is in them, singing:

"To him who sits on the throne and to the Lamb be praise and honor and glory and power, for ever and ever!"

14 The four living creatures said, "Amen," and the elders fell down and worshiped.

By His death on the cross Jesus received authority to open the scroll. Rev 5:12. A third indication of the importance of the message in the scroll

Every creature — All the created intelligent beings of the universe are interested in God's plan for redeeming the lost race of this earth.

IV SATAN'S KINGDOM

THE FIRST FOUR SEALS

Revelation 6:1-8

THE FIRST SEAL

I watched as the Lamb opened the first of the seven seals. Then I heard one of the four living creatures say in a voice like thunder, "Come!" 2 I looked, and there before me was a white horse! Its rider held a bow, and he was given a crown, and he rode out as a conqueror bent on conquest.

THE SECOND SEAL

3 When the Lamb opened the second seal, I heard the second living creature say, "Come!" 4 Then another horse came out, a fiery red one. Its rider was given power to take peace from the earth and to make men slay each other. To him was given a large sword.

THE THIRD SEAL

5 When the Lamb opened the third seal, I heard the third living creature say, "Come!" I looked, and there before me was a

The Lamb, Jesus, now opens to our understanding a description of Satan's kingdom and his objectives.

Voice like thunder — an indication of the importance of the message
White — symbol of purity
Horse — symbol of war; in Biblical history generally seen in connection with battle
Rider — not identified; carried a weapon of war; bent on conquest.

Red — a symbol of sin — Isa 1:18
Rider — not identified; takes away peace; has weapon of war; influences men to kill each other

Revelation 6:1-8 (Cont'd)

black horse! Its rider was holding a pair of scales in his hand. 6 Then I heard what sounded like a voice among the four living creatures, saying, "A quart of wheat for a day's wages, and three quarts of barley for a day's wages, and do not damage the oil and the wine!"

THE FOURTH SEAL

7 When the Lamb opened the fourth seal, I heard the voice of the fourth living creature say, "Come!" 8 I looked, and there before me was a pale horse! Its rider was named Death, and Hades was following close behind him. They were given power over a fourth of the earth to kill by sword, famine and plague, and by the wild beasts of the earth.

Black — opposite of purity; no light or truth in it
Rider — still not identified
Scales — symbol of weighing character — Dan 5:22-28
Wheat and barley — symbols of the Word of God
Day's wages — indicates shortage; symbolic of the Bible being taken from the people
Oil and wine — symbols of the Holy Spirit — was not to be "damaged" or taken away from the faithful people

Pale — symbol of death; truth had been taken from the people
Rider was named Death — symbol of Satan — Rev 20:14, 10
Hades follows rider — Hades are all the forces of evil (See note on Matt 16:18 in NIV Study Bible). Satan is the leader of the forces of evil, therefore the rider, Death, is Satan. It also follows that Satan is the unidentified rider of the first three horses.

The four seals are a description of Satan's attack on the pure apostolic church. He transformed the true church into a counterfeit Christian religion with his errors and false teachings. This apostate church was officially established as the Roman Catholic church in 538 A.D. It then kept the Bible from the people and substituted pagan traditions in place of God's Word.

More information on the time and work of the four seals is presented in <u>The Great Controversy</u> Chapters 2 and 3. See Appendix, p. 102.

The year 538 A.D. is also considered the beginning of the period known as the Dark Ages. Descriptions of this apostate Church-State power are symbolically presented in Revelation 17 (Church) and Revelation 13 (State).

THE WOMAN AND THE BEAST

Revelation 17:1-15

One of the seven angels who had the seven bowls came and said to me, "Come, I will show you the punishment of the great prostitute, who sits on many waters. 2 With her the kings of the earth committed adultery and the inhabitants of the earth were intoxicated with the wine of her adulteries." 3 Then the angel carried me away in the Spirit into a desert. There I saw a woman sitting on a scarlet beast that was covered with blasphemous names and had seven heads and ten horns. 4 The woman was dressed in purple and scarlet, and was glittering with gold, precious stones and pearls. She held a golden cup in her hand, filled with abominable things and the filth of her adulteries. 5 This title was written on her forehead:

Prostitute — symbol of an apostate church or religion
Prostitution, or adultery, is symbolic of corrupting and/or replacing truth with error. Hosea; Eze 23
Waters — symbolic of people — Rev 17:15
Adulteries — Rev 14:8; 18:3
7 heads — Rev 12:3; 13:1; 17:7, 9
10 horns — Dan 7:7, 20, 24; Rev 12:3; 13:1; 17:7, 12
Abominable things, filth of her adulteries — teachings of professed Christian churches that are in error, or that contradict Bible truth — such as:
- *substituting Sunday for the seventh day Sabbath — Ex 20:8-11*
- *teaching that the soul lives on after death — Ecc 9:5, 6*

See Appendix, pp. 103, 104 for additional false teachings.

Revelation 17:1-15 (Cont'd)

MYSTERY
BABYLON THE GREAT
THE MOTHER OF PROSTITUTES
AND OF THE ABOMINATIONS
OF THE EARTH

MYSTERY — preferred reading "This mysterious title was written on her forehead: Babylon . . ."

6 I saw that the woman was drunk with the blood of the saints, the blood of those who bore testimony to Jesus.

When I saw her, I was greatly astonished. 7 Then the angel said to me: "Why are you astonished? I will explain to you the mystery of the woman and of the beast she rides, which has the seven heads and ten horns. 8 The beast, which you saw, once was, now is not, and will come up out of the Abyss and go to his destruction. The inhabitants of the earth whose names have not been written in the book of life from the creation of the world will be astonished when they see the beast, because he once was, now is not, and yet will come.

9 "This calls for a mind with wisdom. The seven heads are seven hills on which the woman sits. 10 They are also seven kings. Five have fallen, one is, the other has not yet come; but when he does come, he must

Saints — Dan 7:19, 21, 25; 8:12, 23-25; Rev 12:13-17

Now is not — Description of the pope being taken captive in 1798 A.D. by French General Berthier. A new pope was appointed in three years, but the political state was not reestablished until 1923 A.D.

We notice that 1798 is just 1,260 years after 538 A.D. It seems reasonable to conclude that this is the 1,260 year period referred to in several references in Daniel and Revelation. Dan 7:25; Rev 12:6, 13-17

Seven Hills — Rome began as a network of seven-hill settlements on the left bank of the Tiber River. Her designation as the

Revelation 17:1-15 (Cont'd)

remain for a little while. 11 The beast who once was, and now is not, is an eighth king. He belongs to the seven and is going to his destruction.

12 "The ten horns you saw are ten kings who have not yet received a kingdom, but who for one hour will receive authority as kings along with the beast. 13 They have one purpose and will give their power and authority to the beast. 14 They will make war against the Lamb, but the Lamb will overcome them because he is Lord of lords and King of kings—and with him will be his called, chosen and faithful followers."

15 Then the angel said to me, "The waters you saw, where the prostitute sits, are peoples, multitudes, nations and languages."

city on seven hills is commonplace among Roman writers (e.g. Virgil, Martial, Cicero)

Make war against the Lamb — See note on Rev 17:6

Compare Dan 2:34, 35, 44, 45; 7:13, 14, 22, 26, 27; 8:23-25; 12:1; Rev 7:1-17; 14:1-5

Where prostitute sits — Rev 17:1

THE BEAST OUT OF THE SEA

Revelation 13:1-10

And the dragon stood on the shore of the sea.
And I saw a beast coming out of the sea. He had ten horns and seven heads, with ten

*Dragon (Satan) — Rev 12:9
Sea (peoples) — Rev 17:15
Beast coming out of the sea —
The Holy Roman Empire coming to power in 538 A.D. Rev 6:1-8*

Revelation 13:1-10 (Cont'd)

crowns on his horns, and on each head a blasphemous name. 2 The beast I saw resembled a leopard, but had feet like those of a bear and a mouth like that of a lion. The dragon gave the beast his power and his throne and great authority. 3 One of the heads of the beast seemed to have had a fatal wound, but the fatal wound had been healed. The whole world was astonished and followed the beast. 4 Men worshiped the dragon because he had given authority to the beast, and they also worshiped the beast and asked, "Who is like the beast? Who can make war against him?"

5 The beast was given a mouth to utter proud words and blasphemies and to exercise his authority for forty-two months. 6 He opened his mouth to blaspheme God, and to slander his name and his dwelling place and those who live in heaven. 7 He was given power to make war against the saints and to conquer them. And he was given authority over every tribe, people, language and nation. 8 All inhabitants of the earth will worship the beast—all whose names have not been written in

Compare with beasts of Dan 7:4-6; Rev 12:3; 17:3
Out of the sea — Rose to power from among nations — Rev 17:15

Fatal wound — Rev 13:12, 14; 17:8, 11
Whole world followed the beast — Compare with the political influence the Roman Catholic Church has in the world today. Dragon (Satan) — Rev 12:9

Utter proud words and blasphemies — Dan 7:8, 20; 8:9-12; Rev 17:3

42 months x 30 days = 1,260 days (years) See note on Dan 7:25; also Dan 12:7; Rev 12:6, 14
War against saints — Dan 7:21, 25; 8:23-25; Rev 12:17; 17:13, 14

Revelation 13:1-10 (Cont'd)

the book of life belonging to the Lamb that was slain from the creation of the world.

9 He who has an ear, let him hear.

10 If anyone is to go into captivity, into captivity he will go. If anyone is to be killed with the sword, with the sword he will be killed. This calls for patient endurance and faithfulness on the part of the saints.

Book of life — Rev 3:5; 20:12, 15; 21:27

Patient endurance — Rev 14:12; Heb 6:12

THE BEAST OUT OF THE EARTH

Revelation 13:11-18

11 Then I saw another beast, coming out of the earth. He had two horns like a lamb, but he spoke like a dragon. 12 He exercised all the authority of the first beast on his behalf, and made the earth and its inhabitants worship the first beast, whose fatal wound had been healed. 13 And he performed great and miraculous signs, even causing fire to come down from heaven to earth in full view of men. 14 Because of

Another beast — A new nation coming to power near the time of the end — 1798 A.D.
Out of earth — did not overthrow another established nation — Compare with Rev 13:1
Two horns of a lamb —
Religious freedom—Protestantism
Political freedom-Republicanism
Fatal wound — In 1798 A.D. French General Berthier took the Pope captive thus giving the beast a fatal wound. The world thought this would destroy the

Revelation 13:11-18 (Cont'd)

the signs he was given power to do on behalf of the first beast, he deceived the inhabitants of the earth. He ordered them to set up an image in honor of the beast who was wounded by the sword and yet lived. 15 He was given power to give breath to the image of the first beast, so that it could speak and cause all who refused to worship the image to be killed. 16 He also forced everyone, small and great, rich and poor, free and slave, to receive a mark on his right hand or on his forehead, 17 so that no one could buy or sell unless he had the mark, which is the name of the beast or the number of his name.

18 This calls for wisdom. If anyone has insight, let him calculate the number of the beast, for it is man's number. His number is 666.

Catholic Church, but the wound healed. See note on Rev 13:3

Wounded — Rev 13:12
Beast, image and mark — Rev 14:9-11
Those who refuse to worship the beast and his image are said to obey the commandments of God. Rev 14:12. The commandments include admonition to "Remember the Sabbath day to keep it holy. . . . the seventh day is the Sabbath of the Lord thy God" Ex 20:8-11

Thus the mark of the beast is seen as the enforcement of a day of worship in opposition to the seventh day Sabbath. The world worships on Sunday, the first day of the week.

This brings to a conclusion the objectives of Satan and the beast powers that work with him. Their final objective is to destroy all commandment—keeping saints.
Man's number — 666

Revelation 13:11-18 (Cont'd)

Pope's Title

V	=	5
I	=	1
C	=	100
A	=	0
R	=	0
I	=	1
U	=	5
S	=	0
F	=	0
I	=	1
L	=	50
I	=	1
I	=	1
D	=	500
E	=	0
I	=	1

Man's Number — 666

A title given to the pope is "Vicarius Filii Dei" which means vicegerent of the Son of God.

Roman numeral values

I	=	1
U (V)	=	5
L	=	50
C	=	100
D	=	500

VICARIUS	=	112
FILII	=	53
DEI	=	501
		666

Now that we have discovered the objective of Satan and his beast powers, we shall next turn to a study of Christ's messages to His followers, the saints. These messages begin in Revelation Chapter 1.

V CHRIST'S KINGDOM

CHRIST INTRODUCES HIMSELF

Revelation 1:4-20

John, To the seven churches in the province of Asia:

Grace and peace to you from him who is, and who was, and who is to come, and from the seven spirits before his throne, 5 and from Jesus Christ, who is the faithful witness, the firstborn from the dead, and the ruler of the kings of the earth.

To him who loves us and has freed us from our sins by his blood, 6 and has made us to be a kingdom and priests to serve his God and Father — to him be glory and power for ever and ever! Amen.

7 Look, he is coming with the clouds, and every eye will see him, even those who pierced him; and all the peoples of the earth will mourn because of him. So shall it be! Amen.

8 "I am the Alpha and the Omega," says the Lord God, "who is, and who was, and who is to come, the Almighty."

Him who is, was, etc. —
God the Father — Rev 4:3-11
Seven spirits — Holy Spirit — Rev 4:5
Jesus Christ — God the Son
All three members of the Godhead are involved in saving fallen man.
Jesus gave His life for you and me.
Notice that the setting here in Chapter 1 is the same as in Chapter 4. The messages about the beasts and the messages to the saints come from God on His throne in the Holy Place of the sanctuary in Heaven at the time when Jesus ascended to Heaven. Rev 5:6
Look, he is coming . . . every eye will see Him — Second Advent — Acts 1:11; 1 Thess 4:16-18

Revelation 1:4-20 (Cont'd)

9 I, John, your brother and companion in the suffering and kingdom and patient endurance that are ours in Jesus, was on the island of Patmos because of the word of God and the testimony of Jesus. 10 On the Lord's Day I was in the Spirit, and I heard behind me a loud voice like a trumpet, 11 which said: "Write on a scroll what you see and send it to the seven churches: to Ephesus, Smyrna, Pergamum, Thyatira, Sardis, Philadelphia and Laodicea."

12 I turned around to see the voice that was speaking to me. And when I turned I saw seven golden lamp stands, 13 and among the lamp stands was someone "like a son of man," dressed in a robe reaching down to his feet and with a golden sash around his chest. 14 His head and hair were white like wool, as white as snow, and his eyes were like blazing fire. 15 His feet were like bronze glowing in a furnace, and his voice was like the sound of rushing waters. 16 In his right hand he held seven stars, and out of his mouth came a sharp double-edged sword. His face was like the sun shining in all its brilliance.

The disciple, John

The Lord's Day — Mark 2:27, 28 — Seventh-day Sabbath — Christians did not begin using Sunday as a day of worship for over 100 years after John was given this vision.

Golden lamp stands — an article of furniture in the Holy Place of the sanctuary on earth which was a copy of the heavenly sanctuary. Ex 40:24; Heb 9:2, 23, 24; Rev 4:5
Description of Christ as our High Priest
Jesus begins His ministry in the Holy Place of the sanctuary in Heaven.

Double-edged sword — Word of God — Heb 4:12

Revelation 1:4-20 (Cont'd)

17 When I saw him, I fell at his feet as though dead. Then he placed his right hand on me and said: "Do not be afraid. I am the First and the Last. 18 I am the Living One; I was dead, and behold I am alive for ever and ever! And I hold the keys of death and Hades.

19 "Write, therefore, what you have seen, what is now and what will take place later. 20 The mystery of the seven stars that you saw in my right hand and of the seven golden lamp stands is this: The seven stars are the angels of the seven churches, and the seven lamp stands are the seven churches.

I am the Living One — Christ's death, burial and resurrection Compare Rev 5:6
Keys of death and Hades — Christ has control over Satan and the fallen angels. Rev 6:8; Mt 16:18
Seven stars and seven angels — Symbols of church leaders

In summary, chapters 1, 4 and 5 are a description of the beginning of Christ's ministry in the Holy Place of the heavenly sanctuary.

TO THE CHURCH IN EPHESUS

Revelation 2:1-7

"To the angel of the church in Ephesus write:
These are the words of him who holds the seven stars in his right hand and walks among the seven golden lamp stands: 2 I know your deeds, your hard work and your perseverance.

Chapters 2 and 3 are messages from Christ to His church to guide them safely through the war (Rev 12:17) to the Holy City.
Seven stars — Rev 1:16, 20
Lamp stands — Rev 1:12, 13, 20

Revelation 2:1-7 (Cont'd)

I know that you cannot tolerate wicked men, that you have tested those who claim to be apostles but are not, and have found them false. 3 You have persevered and have endured hardships for my name, and have not grown weary.

4 Yet I hold this against you: You have forsaken your first love. 5 Remember the height from which you have fallen! Repent and do the things you did at first. If you do not repent, I will come to you and remove your lamp stand from its place. 6 But you have this in your favor: You hate the practices of the Nicolaitans, which I also hate.

7 He who has an ear, let him hear what the Spirit says to the churches. To him who overcomes, I will give the right to eat from the tree of life, which is in the paradise of God.

Characteristics of the saints —
  Cannot tolerate wicked men
  Test claims of apostles
  Recognize false claims
  Persevere
  Endure
  Do not grow weary

Characteristic of professed Christians —
  Forsake first love

Requires repentance to be saved

Nicolaitans — brought idolatry and immorality into the church; some promoted teaching of Balaam, others of Jezebel
Listen to the Holy Spirit

Saints reward — right to eat from the tree of life

TO THE CHURCH IN SMYRNA

Revelation 2:8-11

8 "To the angel of the church in Smyrna write:

Revelation 2:8-11 (Cont'd)

These are the words of him who is the First and the Last, who died and came to life again. 9 I know your afflictions and your poverty — yet you are rich! I know the slander of those who say they are Jews and are not, but are a synagogue of Satan. 10 Do not be afraid of what you are about to suffer. I tell you, the devil will put some of you in prison to test you, and you will suffer persecution for ten days. Be faithful, even to the point of death, and I will give you the crown of life.
11 He who has an ear, let him hear what the Spirit says to the churches. He who overcomes will not be hurt at all by the second death.

First and Last — Rev 1:17
Came to life again — Rev 1:18

Synagogue of Satan — 2 Cor 11:13-15 — *professed Christian churches who do not obey the Word*
Do not be afraid — Isa 51:7

Persecution — Dan 7:21, 23; 8:23-25; Rev 12:17; 17:13, 14

Listen to the Holy Spirit

Second death — Rev 20:6, 14; 21:8

TO THE CHURCH IN PERGAMUM

Revelation 2:12-17

12 "To the angel of the church in Pergamum write:
These are the words of him who has the sharp, double-edged sword. 13 I know where you live — where Satan has his throne.

Double-edged sword — Rev 1:16; Heb 4:12

Revelation 2:12-17 (Cont'd)

Yet you remain true to my name. You did not renounce your faith in me, even in the days of Antipas, my faithful witness, who was put to death in your city — where Satan lives.

14 Nevertheless, I have a few things against you: You have people there who hold to the teaching of Balaam, who taught Balak to entice the Israelites to sin by eating food sacrificed to idols and by committing sexual immorality. 15 Likewise you also have those who hold to the teaching of the Nicolaitans. 16 Repent therefore! Otherwise, I will soon come to you and will fight against them with the sword of my mouth.

17 He who has an ear, let him hear what the Spirit says to the churches. To him who overcomes, I will give some of the hidden manna. I will also give him a white stone with a new name written on it, known only to him who receives it.

Commendations to the true Christian

Warnings and counsel to professed Christians who do not obey the Word of God

Nicolaitans — Rev 2:6 — Their influence seems stronger in the Pergamum Church than in the earlier Ephesian Church.
Requires repentance
Sword — Rev 2:12
Listen to the Holy Spirit

Manna — Jn 6:48-51

New name — Isa 62:1-3

TO THE CHURCH IN THYATIRA

Revelation 2:18-29

18 "To the angel of the church in Thyatira write:

These are the words of the Son of God, whose eyes are like blazing fire and whose feet are like burnished bronze. 19 I know your deeds, your love and faith, your service and perseverance, and that you are now doing more than you did at first.

20 Nevertheless, I have this against you: You tolerate that woman Jezebel, who calls herself a prophetess. By her teaching she misleads my servants into sexual immorality and the eating of food sacrificed to idols. 21 I have given her time to repent of her immorality, but she is unwilling. 22 So I will cast her on a bed of suffering, and I will make those who commit adultery with her suffer intensely, unless they repent of her ways. 23 I will strike her children dead. Then all the churches will know that I am he who searches hearts and minds, and I will repay each of you according to your deeds. 24 Now I say to the rest of you in Thyatira, to

Eyes like blazing fire — feet like bronze — Rev 1:14, 15

Commendations to true Christians

Tolerate Jezebel — The Nicolaitan teaching was first hated, but now it is tolerated — Rev 2:6, 15
Sexual immorality — both literal and spiritual adultery — Hosea; Ezek 23

Repentance required to be saved

Revelation 2:18-29 (Cont'd)

you who do not hold to her teaching and have not learned Satan's so-called deep secrets (I will not impose any other burden on you): 25 Only hold on to what you have until I come.

Counsel for true Christians

26 To him who overcomes and does my will to the end, I will give authority over the nations —

Reward of true Christians

27 'He will rule them with an iron scepter, he will dash them to pieces like pottery' — just as I have received authority from my Father. 28 I will also give him the morning star. 29 He who has an ear, let him hear what the Spirit says to the churches.

Morning star — Rev 22:16

Listen to the Holy Spirit

TO THE CHURCH IN SARDIS

Revelation 3:1-6

"To the angel of the church in Sardis write:

These are the words of him who holds the seven spirits of God and the seven stars. I know your deeds; you have a reputation of being alive, but you are dead. 2 Wake up! Strengthen what remains and is about to die, for I have not found your deeds complete in

Seven spirits, seven stars — Rev 1:4, 16, 20
Reputation of being alive — that is they are called Christians but do not the work of Christ
Wake up! — God requires His saints to be faithful and diligent workers.

Revelation 3:1-6 (Cont'd)

the sight of my God. 3 Remember, therefore, what you have received and heard; obey it, and repent. But if you do not wake up, I will come like a thief, and you will not know at what time I will come to you.

4 Yet you have a few people in Sardis who have not soiled their clothes. They will walk with me, dressed in white, for they are worthy. 5 He who overcomes will, like them, be dressed in white. I will never blot out his name from the book of life, but will acknowledge his name before my Father and his angels. 6 He who has an ear, let him hear what the Spirit says to the churches.

Requires repentance to be saved
Come like a thief — 1 Thes 5:2; 2 Pet 3:10; Rev 16:15

Few people — few Christians have allowed Jesus to wash away their sins with His blood
Dressed in white — without sin, covered with the righteousness of Christ — Rev 3:5, 18; Isa 1:18; Rev 6:11; 7:9, 13, 14; 19:8, 14

Book of life — Rev 13:8

Listen to the Holy Spirit

TO THE CHURCH IN PHILADELPHIA

Revelation 3:7-13

7 "To the angel of the church in Philadelphia write:

These are the words of him who is holy and true, who holds the key of David. What he

Holy and true — Mark 1:24; 1 Jn 5:20

Revelation 3:7-13 (Cont'd)

opens no one can shut, and what he shuts no one can open. 8 I know your deeds. See, I have placed before you an open door that no one can shut. I know that you have little strength, yet you have kept my word and have not denied my name. 9 I will make those who are of the synagogue of Satan, who claim to be Jews though they are not, but are liars—I will make them come and fall down at your feet and acknowledge that I have loved you. 10 Since you have kept my command to endure patiently, I will also keep you from the hour of trial that is going to come upon the whole world to test those who live on the earth.
11 I am coming soon. Hold on to what you have, so that no one will take your crown. 12 Him who overcomes I will make a pillar in the temple of my God. Never again will he leave it. I will write on him the name of my God and the name of the city of my God, the new Jerusalem, which is coming down out of heaven from my God; and I will also write on him my new name. 13 He who has an ear, let him hear what the Spirit says to the churches.

What He opens . . . shuts — Description of Jesus moving from the Holy to the Most Holy Place in the sanctuary in heaven on October 22, 1844 to begin the investigative judgment — Dan 7:9, 10, 13; Mal 3:1-3
Little strength — the advent believers at this time were few in number
Synagogue of Satan — Rev 2:9

Hour of trial . . . to test — Rev 13:15-17; 14:9-12

Coming soon — 1 Thes 4:13-18

New Jerusalem — Rev 21:2, 10

Listen to the Holy Spirit

TO THE CHURCH IN LAODICEA

Revelation 3:14-22

14 "To the angel of the church in Laodicea write:

These are the words of the Amen, the faithful and true witness, the ruler of God's creation. 15 I know your deeds, that you are neither cold nor hot. I wish you were either one or the other! 16 So, because you are lukewarm — neither hot nor cold — I am about to spit you out of my mouth. 17 You say, 'I am rich; I have acquired wealth and do not need a thing.' But you do not realize that you are wretched, pitiful, poor, blind and naked. 18 I counsel you to buy from me gold refined in the fire, so you can become rich; and white clothes to wear, so you can cover your shameful nakedness; and salve to put on your eyes, so you can see.

19 Those whom I love I rebuke and discipline. So be earnest, and repent. 20 Here I

Amen — Christ — 2 Cor 1:20
Faithful and true — Rev 1:5; 3:7
Creation — Gen 1; Ex 20:8-11; Rev 14:6, 7

Lukewarm — symbolic of a state of indifference and disobedience to the ten commandments and the Word of God

Do not realize — the status of the professed Christian is pathetic

I counsel — Jesus still pleads with them

White clothes — Rev 3:4

Requires repentance to be saved

Revelation 3:14-22 (Cont'd)

am! I stand at the door and knock. If anyone hears my voice and opens the door, I will come in and eat with him, and he with me.

21 To him who overcomes, I will give the right to sit with me on my throne, just as I overcame and sat down with my Father on his throne. 22 He who has an ear, let him hear what the Spirit says to the churches."

Stand at the door — The Word of God (Jesus — John 1:1, 14) is ready to enter any heart (mind) who will receive Him, the Way, the Truth and the Life.

Sit on my throne — For a description of the glory of God on the throne see Rev 4, 5 and Rev 21:5

Listen to the Holy Spirit

The messages of Jesus Christ to the seven churches are filled with warnings, counsel, guidance and rewards for Christians living in the time of the end. From the time the Ephesian Church lost its "first love" to the "indifference" of the Laodicean Church there has been a gradual drifting away from God and purity of character. At the present time there are few who obey the law of God and remain faithful to Jesus. Rev 14:12.

Dear Reader, where do you stand? Are you one with Christ in obedience to the commandments, or are you following Satan, the dragon?

VI THE EVERLASTING GOSPEL AND ITS COUNTERFEIT

THE TWO WITNESSES

Revelation 11:1-13

I was given a reed like a measuring rod and was told, "Go and measure the temple of God and the altar, and count the worshipers there. 2 But exclude the outer court; do not measure it, because it has been given to the Gentiles. They will trample on the holy city for 42 months. 3 And I will give power to my two witnesses, and they will prophesy for 1,260 days, clothed in sackcloth." 4 These are the two olive trees and the two lamp stands that stand before the Lord of the earth. 5 If anyone tries to harm them, fire comes from their mouths and devours their enemies. This is how anyone who wants to harm them must die. 6 These men have power to shut up the sky so that it will not rain during the time they are prophesying; and they have power to turn the waters into blood and to strike

The focus of our attention now shifts to the dispersion of the gospel, near the end of the Dark Ages. This judgment hour message grows in power and brilliance to prepare God's people for the second coming of Jesus when the war between Christ and Satan will be forever settled.

42 months — 1,260 years — Dan 7:25

Two witnesses — Old and New Testaments — Acts 10:43; Rom 3:21; Luke 24:27; Rev 1:1, 2

Clothed in sackcloth — symbol of the suppression of the Bible by the Roman church during the 1,260-year period

Two olive trees and lamp stands — Ps 119:105

Harm them — Rev 22:18, 19

Shut up the sky — 1 Ki 17:1

Waters into blood — Ex 7:14-24

Revelation 11:1-13 (Cont'd)

the earth with every kind of plague as often as they want.

7 Now when they have finished their testimony, the beast that comes up from the Abyss will attack them, and overpower and kill them. 8 Their bodies will lie in the street of the great city, which is figuratively called Sodom and Egypt, where also their Lord was crucified. 9 For three and a half days men from every people, tribe, language and nation will gaze on their bodies and refuse them burial. 10 The inhabitants of the earth will gloat over them and will celebrate by sending each other gifts, because these two prophets had tormented those who live on the earth.

11 But after the three and a half days a breath of life from God entered them, and they stood on their feet, and terror struck those who saw them. 12 Then they heard a loud voice from heaven saying to them, "Come up here." And they went up to heaven in a cloud, while their enemies looked on.

13 At that very hour there was a severe earthquake and a tenth of the city collapsed.

Beast — symbol of a nation — Dan 7:17
Sodom — Known for its licentiousness — Gen 19:4-9
Egypt — known for its defiance of God — Ex 5:2
These are two characteristics of the nation that would attempt to destroy the two witnesses.
Three and one-half days — Prophetic years — In 1793 the French Assembly decreed to abolish the Christian religion and destroy the Bible. Just three and one-half years later the same assembly rescinded this decree.
Compare history of France and her persecution of Christians.
- *St. Bartholomew Massacre*
- *French Revolution and actions against the Bible*
- *The "Reign of Terror"*

Come up here — A description of God elevating the importance of the Scriptures in the eyes of men. This is shown in the founding of the British and Foreign Bible Society in 1804 and the American Bible Society in 1816, also in the organization of missionary societies.

Revelation 11:1-13 (Cont'd)

Seven thousand people were killed in the earthquake, and the survivors were terrified and gave glory to the God of heaven.

THE ANGEL AND THE SCROLL

Revelation 10

Then I saw another mighty angel coming down from heaven. He was robed in a cloud, with a rainbow above his head; his face was like the sun, and his legs were like fiery pillars. 2 He was holding a little scroll, which lay open in his hand. He planted his right foot on the sea and his left foot on the land, 3 and he gave a loud shout like the roar of a lion. When he shouted, the voices of the seven thunders spoke. 4 And when the seven thunders spoke, I was about to write; but I heard a voice from heaven say, "Seal up what the seven thunders have said and do not write it down." 5 Then the angel I had seen standing on the sea and on the

Today millions of copies of the Bible are distributed every year. Translations are available in nearly all languages of the world.

The gospel is going to the world via radio, shortwave radio and television. Never in the history of mankind has there been such widespread availability of the Word of God throughout the world.

Mighty angel — Jesus Christ
  Robe — Rev 1:13
  Rainbow — Eze 1:28; Rev 4:3
  Face like the sun — Rev 1:16
  Legs like fire — Eze 1:27; Rev 1:15
Foot on sea and land — Symbol of the wide extent of the proclamation of the message; also denotes Christ's supreme power and authority over the world
Loud shout — indicates importance of the message

Revelation 10 (Cont'd)

land raised his right hand to heaven. 6 And he swore by him who lives for ever and ever, who created the heavens and all that is in them, the earth and all that is in it, and the sea and all that is in it, and said, "There will be no more delay! 7 But in the days when the seventh angel is about to sound his trumpet, the mystery of God will be accomplished, just as he announced to his servants the prophets."

8 Then the voice that I had heard from heaven spoke to me once more: "Go, take the scroll that lies open in the hand of the angel who is standing on the sea and on the land."

9 So I went to the angel and asked him to give me the little scroll. He said to me, "Take it and eat it. It will turn your stomach sour, but in your mouth it will be as sweet as honey." 10 I took the little scroll from the angel's hand and ate it. It tasted as sweet as honey in my mouth, but when I had eaten it, my stomach turned sour. 11 Then I was told, "You must prophesy again about many peoples, nations, languages and kings."

Created — Gen 1 and 2; Ex 20:8-11; Rev 14:6, 7

Seventh angel sounds trumpet — Rev 11:15-19 (time for judging has come — Rev 11:18) This places the setting for this chapter in 1844 A.D. — See note on Dan 8:14; Rev 14:6, 7

Eat it — Jesus is the living bread. — Jn 1:1, 14; 6:25-58
Sweet as honey — The advent awakening of the 1830's and 1840's was a bright and joyous hope.
Stomach turned sour — When Jesus did not come in Oct. 1844 there was great disappointment.
Prophesy again — The message of the three angels in Rev 14:6-12 is to be proclaimed to the world from 1844 to the end of time.

SIGNS REVEAL JUDGMENT TIME

Revelation 6:9-13

9 When he opened the fifth seal, I saw under the altar the souls of those who had been slain because of the word of God and the testimony they had maintained. 10 They called out in a loud voice, "How long, Sovereign Lord, holy and true, until you judge the inhabitants of the earth and avenge our blood?" 11 Then each of them was given a white robe, and they were told to wait a little longer, until the number of their fellow servants and brothers who were to be killed as they had been was completed.

12 I watched as he opened the sixth seal. There was a great earthquake. The sun turned black like sackcloth made of goat hair, the whole moon turned blood red, 13 and the stars in the sky fell to earth, as late figs drop from a fig tree when shaken by a strong wind.

A symbolic description of the saints during the 1,260-year period of the Dark Ages, 538 A.D. to 1798 A.D. under the persecution of the Holy Roman Empire. Rev. 12:14-17

Saints inquire when judgment will begin

White robe — Rev 3:4, 5; 7:9
Brothers . . . to be killed — persecution will show its ugly head again before Jesus comes — Rev 13:15-17
The sixth seal gives signs warning that the coming of the judgment is near — Mt 24:29, 30
Great earthquake — Fulfilled 1755 A.D. — known as the Lisbon Earthquake
Sun darkened and moon turned to blood — Fulfilled May 19, 1780
Falling stars — Fulfilled Nov 13, 1833
See also Great Controversy 304-308, 333, 334
See Appendix, p. 102

THE THREE ANGELS' MESSAGES

THE FIRST ANGEL'S MESSAGE

Revelation 14:6, 7

6 Then I saw another angel flying in midair, and he had the eternal gospel to proclaim to those who live on the earth — to every nation, tribe, language and people. 7 He said in a loud voice, "Fear God and give him glory, because the hour of his judgment has come. Worship him who made the heavens, the earth, the sea and the springs of water."

Gospel — death, burial and resurrection of Christ to cleanse us from sin
To every nation — to be given to all the world

Hour of judgment — Judgment began in 1844 — Dan 8:14
Worship him who made — Gen 1 and 2; Ex 20:8-11
Compare with objectives of the beast in Rev 13:15-17

Revelation 11:19

19 Then God's temple in heaven was opened, and within his temple was seen the ark of his covenant. And there came flashes of lightning, rumblings, peals of thunder, an earthquake and a great hailstorm.

God's temple — Dan 7:9, 10
Another view of the judgment which began in 1844

Revelation 19:1-10

After this I heard what sounded like the roar of a great multitude in heaven shouting:

These verses describe the opening scene of the judgment which began in 1844. This judgment is the investigative judgment.

Revelation 19:1-10 (Cont'd)

"Hallelujah! Salvation and glory and power belong to our God, 2 for true and just are his judgments. He has condemned the great prostitute who corrupted the earth by her adulteries. He has avenged on her the blood of his servants." 3 And again they shouted: "Hallelujah! The smoke from her goes up for ever and ever."

4 The twenty-four elders and the four living creatures fell down and worshiped God, who was seated on the throne. And they cried: "Amen, Hallelujah!"

5 Then a voice came from the throne, saying: "Praise our God, all you his servants, you who fear him, both small and great!"

6 Then I heard what sounded like a great multitude, like the roar of rushing waters and like loud peals of thunder, shouting: "Hallelujah! For our Lord God Almighty reigns. 7 Let us rejoice and be glad and give him glory! For the wedding of the Lamb has come, and his bride has made herself ready. 8 Fine linen, bright and clean, was given her to wear." (Fine linen stands for the righteous acts of the saints.)

9 Then the angel said to me,

Prostitute — Rev 17:1-6

Seated on the throne — Dan 7:9, 10, 13, 14; Rev 4

Wedding has come — During the investigative judgment the saints are to prepare for the wedding.

Revelation 19:1-10 (Cont'd)

"Write: 'Blessed are those who are invited to the wedding supper of the Lamb!' " And he added, "These are the true words of God."

10 At this I fell at his feet to worship him. But he said to me, "Do not do it! I am a fellow servant with you and with your brothers who hold to the testimony of Jesus. Worship God! For the testimony of Jesus is the spirit of prophecy."

Blessed — Rev 14:12, 13
Invited to wedding — Mt 22:1-14
Wedding supper — Takes place after the judgment is completed — Mt 25:6-10

Testimony of Jesus — Rev 12:17

THE SECOND ANGEL'S MESSAGE

Revelation 14:8

8 A second angel followed and said, "Fallen! Fallen is Babylon the Great, which made all the nations drink the maddening wine of her adulteries."

Churches are described as fallen when they reject the truths of the Bible
Adulteries — Rev 17:1-6; 19:2
See note on Rev 17:2, 4

Revelation 18:1-8

After this I saw another angel coming down from heaven. He had great authority, and the earth was illuminated by his splendor. 2 With a mighty voice he shouted:

"Fallen! Fallen is Babylon the

This angel is not one of the three angels in Rev 14, but another angel whom God sends to add emphasis to the second angel's message. The "fall of Babylon" is to be proclaimed with greater force as the investigative judgment nears its culmination and probation is about to close.

Revelation 18:1-8 (Cont'd)

Great! She has become a home for demons and a haunt for every evil spirit, a haunt for every unclean and detestable bird. 3 For all the nations have drunk the maddening wine of her adulteries. The kings of the earth committed adultery with her, and the merchants of the earth grew rich from her excessive luxuries."

4 Then I heard another voice from heaven say: "Come out of her, my people, so that you will not share in her sins, so that you will not receive any of her plagues; 5 for her sins are piled up to heaven, and God has remembered her crimes.

6 Give back to her as she has given; pay her back double for what she has done. Mix her a double portion from her own cup. 7 Give her as much torture and grief as the glory and luxury she gave herself. In her heart she boasts, 'I sit as queen; I am not a widow, and I will never mourn.'

8 Therefore in one day her plagues will overtake her: death, mourning and famine. She will be consumed by fire, for mighty is the Lord God who judges her."

This is the final warning to the people of the world to come out of Babylon (the fallen churches who have rejected the commandments of God)
Haunt for evil spirits —
Rev 16:13-16
Unclean and detestable bird — symbolic of teachings and traditions of the fallen churches that are not in harmony with Bible truth
Wine of her adulteries — symbolic of false teachings — Rev 14:8; 17:4
Come out of her My people —last call of mercy to God's faithful people
Probation is soon to close

Plagues are soon to fall and Babylon will be destroyed — Dan 2:44, 45; 7:26, 27; 8:23-25; 12:1, 2

THE THIRD ANGEL'S MESSAGE

Revelation 14:9-13

9 A third angel followed them and said in a loud voice: "If anyone worships the beast and his image and receives his mark on the forehead or on the hand, 10 he, too, will drink of the wine of God's fury, which has been poured full strength into the cup of his wrath. He will be tormented with burning sulfur in the presence of the holy angels and of the Lamb. 11 And the smoke of their torment rises for ever and ever. There is no rest day or night for those who worship the beast and his image, or for anyone who receives the mark of his name." 12 This calls for patient endurance on the part of the saints who obey God's commandments and remain faithful to Jesus.

13 Then I heard a voice from heaven say, "Write: Blessed are the dead who die in the Lord from now on. "

"Yes," says the Spirit, "they will rest from their labor, for their deeds will follow them."

Beast, image and mark — Rev 13:14-18

God will destroy all who follow the beast and receive his mark.

Smoke rises forever — Rev 19:3; Jude 7; 2 Pet 3:7

Beast and his image — Rev 13:14-17
Mark — Rev 13:16, 17

Saints — Do not worship the beast or receive his mark; obey God's commandments — Ex 20:3-17; remember to keep holy the seventh day Sabbath, which is the fourth commandment; remain faithful to Jesus
The mark of the beast is then seen as Sunday worship enforced by the beast. This is in direct opposition to the seventh day Sabbath of the Creator.

144,000 Sealed

Revelation 7:1-8

After this I saw four angels standing at the four corners of the earth, holding back the four winds of the earth to prevent any wind from blowing on the land or on the sea or on any tree. 2 Then I saw another angel coming up from the east, having the seal of the living God. He called out in a loud voice to the four angels who had been given power to harm the land and the sea: 3 "Do not harm the land or the sea or the trees until we put a seal on the foreheads of the servants of our God." 4 Then I heard the number of those who were sealed: 144,000 from all the tribes of Israel.

5 From the tribe of Judah 12,000 were sealed, from the tribe of Reuben 12,000, from the tribe of Gad 12,000,

6 from the tribe of Asher 12,000, from the tribe of Naphtali 12,000, from the tribe of Manasseh 12,000,

7 from the tribe of Simeon 12,000, from the tribe of Levi 12,000, from the tribe of Issachar 12,000,

8 from the tribe of Zebulun 12,000, from the tribe of Joseph 12,000, from the tribe of Benjamin 12,000.

Winds — A symbol of strife and destruction — Jer 49:36

Do not harm — The obedient, faithful saints are protected by God.
We — Angels do the sealing work.
Seal on foreheads — symbolic of settling into the truth of God, both intellectually and spiritually
144,000 — It is not clear whether this number is literal or symbolic.
Tribes of Israel — The meaning of the tribes is uncertain.

THREE EVIL SPIRITS

Revelation 16:13-16

13 Then I saw three evil spirits that looked like frogs; they came out of the mouth of the dragon, out of the mouth of the beast and out of the mouth of the false prophet. 14 They are spirits of demons performing miraculous signs, and they go out to the kings of the whole world, to gather them for the battle on the great day of God Almighty.

15 "Behold, I come like a thief! Blessed is he who stays awake and keeps his clothes with him, so that he may not go naked and be shamefully exposed."

16 Then they gathered the kings together to the place that in Hebrew is called Armageddon.

CLOSING REMARKS OF GOD THE FATHER

Revelation 21:5-8

5 He who was seated on the throne said, "I am making everything new!" Then he said, "Write this down, for these words are trustworthy and true."

Evil spirits — Rev. 12:9
Satan attempts to deceive people by sending three evil spirits with messages to the world to counteract the message of the three angels of Rev 14:6-12.
Modern spiritualism began with the mysterious rapping in the home of the Fox sisters in 1848. It has developed widely in many forms since that time.

Dragon — Rev 12 and 13
Beast — Rev 13
False prophet — People and/or churches who teach error in place of Bible truth — Mt 24:24; Rev 19:20; See note on Rev 17:1

The three angels of Rev 14 prepare a people to live forever with Jesus.
The three evil angels of Rev 16 prepare the rest of the world for the battle of Armageddon and eternal death.

Seated on the throne — Rev 4:2, 3
"Write this down" — Rev 1:1-3

Revelation 21:5-8 (Cont'd)

6 He said to me: "It is done. I am the Alpha and the Omega, the Beginning and the End. To him who is thirsty I will give to drink without cost from the spring of the water of life. 7 He who overcomes will inherit all this, and I will be his God and he will be my son. 8 But the cowardly, the unbelieving, the vile, the murderers, the sexually immoral, those who practice magic arts, the idolaters and all liars—their place will be in the fiery lake of burning sulfur. This is the second death."

"It is done" — The end has come; probation has closed.

He who overcomes — will inherit eternal life — Rev 14:12, 13

The unfaithful go to the lake of fire and the second death. — Rev 20:14

CLOSING REMARKS OF JESUS

Revelation 22:7, 12-16, 20

7 "Behold, I am coming soon! Blessed is he who keeps the words of the prophecy in this book."

12 "Behold, I am coming soon! My reward is with me, and I will give to everyone according to what he has done.

13 "I am the Alpha and the Omega, the First and the Last, the Beginning and the End.

Those who obey are blessed.

Second advent — First advent occurred when Jesus was born in Bethlehem — Lk 2:1-20; Mt 1:18-25

Revelation 22:12-16, 20 (Cont'd)

14 "Blessed are those who wash their robes, that they may have the right to the tree of life and may go through the gates into the city. 15 Outside are the dogs, those who practice magic arts, the sexually immoral, the murderers, the idolaters and everyone who loves and practices falsehood.
16 "I, Jesus, have sent my angel to give you this testimony for the churches. I am the Root and the Offspring of David, and the bright and Morning Star."
20 . . . "Yes, I am coming soon."

Saints enter the Holy City, the new Jerusalem — Rev 21:2

The unrighteous are kept outside the city.

Sent my angel — Rev 1:1

Testimony for the churches — Rev 1:2, 9-11; Rev 2 and 3

CLOSING REMARKS OF THE HOLY SPIRIT

Revelation 22:17

17 The Spirit and the bride say, "Come!" And let him who hears say, "Come!" Whoever is thirsty, let him come; and whoever wishes, let him take the free gift of the water of life.

The Spirit — The Holy Spirit — Rev 1:4; 4:5
Bride — New Jerusalem — Rev 21:2, 10 — a symbol of all the intelligent beings and angels of the universe who have, since Satan was cast out of heaven, been watching the controversy between Christ and Satan.
They all invite us to come to Jesus.
Water of life — Rev 21:6

CLOSING REMARKS OF JOHN

Revelation 22:8-11, 18-21

8 I, John, am the one who heard and saw these things. And when I had heard and seen them, I fell down to worship at the feet of the angel who had been showing them to me. 9 But he said to me, "Do not do it! I am a fellow servant with you and with your brothers the prophets and of all who keep the words of this book. Worship God!"

10 Then he told me, "Do not seal up the words of the prophecy of this book, because the time is near. 11 Let him who does wrong continue to do wrong; let him who is vile continue to be vile; let him who does right continue to do right; and let him who is holy continue to be holy."

18 I warn everyone who hears the words of the prophecy of this book: If anyone adds anything to them, God will add to him the plagues described in this book. 19 And if anyone

"Do not seal up the words" — The book of Revelation is to be understood.

Probation has closed; each individual's decision about Christ is now final.

God holds everyone responsible for how he believes and uses the Word of God.

Plagues — Rev 16

Revelation 22: 18-21 (Cont'd)

takes words away from this book of prophecy, God will take away from him his share in the tree of life and in the holy city, which are described in this book.

20 He who testifies to these things says, "Yes, I am coming soon."

Amen. Come, Lord Jesus.

21 The grace of the Lord Jesus be with God's people. Amen.

Tree of life — Gen 2:9; Rev 22:2

John's closing prayer.

VII THE CONCLUSION OF THE CONTROVERSY

SEVEN ANGELS WITH SEVEN PLAGUES

Revelation 15:1, 5-8; 16:1

I saw in heaven another great and marvelous sign: seven angels with the seven last plagues — last, because with them God's wrath is completed.

5 After this I looked and in heaven the temple, that is, the tabernacle of the Testimony, was opened. 6 Out of the temple came the seven angels with the seven plagues. They were dressed in clean, shining linen and wore golden sashes around their chests. 7 Then one of the four living creatures gave to the seven angels seven golden bowls filled with the wrath of God, who lives for ever and ever. 8 And the temple was filled with smoke from the glory of God and from his power, and no one could enter the temple until the seven plagues of the seven angels were completed.

Seven last plagues — Ex 7:14 to 12:36 tell about the ten plagues that fell on Egypt when that nation stood in defiance of the God of Heaven.

Tabernacle of the Testimony — the Most Holy Place where the ten commandments are kept in the ark — Heb 9:3, 4

Wrath of God — Rev 14:9, 10

No one in temple — judgment is finished

Revelation 16:1 (Cont'd)

Then I heard a loud voice from the temple saying to the seven angels, "Go, pour out the seven bowls of God's wrath on the earth."

THE FIRST PLAGUE

Revelation 16:2

2 The first angel went and poured out his bowl on the land, and ugly and painful sores broke out on the people who had the mark of the beast and worshiped his image.

Mark of beast — Rev 13:14-17; 14:9-11

THE SECOND PLAGUE

Revelation 16:3

3 The second angel poured out his bowl on the sea, and it turned into blood like that of a dead man, and every living thing in the sea died.

THE THIRD PLAGUE

Revelation 16:4-7

4 The third angel poured out his bowl on the rivers and springs of water, and they became blood. 5 Then I heard the angel in charge of the waters say:

"You are just in these judgments, you who are and who were, the Holy One, because you have so judged; 6 for they have shed the blood of your saints and prophets, and you have given them blood to drink as they deserve." 7 And I heard the altar respond:

"Yes, Lord God Almighty, true and just are your judgments."

Rivers to blood — Ex 7:14-24

You who are — Rev 1:4, 8

Shed blood of saints — Dan 7:21, 25; 8:12; Rev 17:6

Altar — Rev 6:9

THE FOURTH PLAGUE

Revelation 16:8, 9

8 The fourth angel poured out his bowl on the sun, and the sun was given power to scorch people with fire. 9 They were seared by the intense heat and they cursed the name of God, who had control over these plagues, but they refused to repent and glorify him.

The heat will be especially painful because there is no water, only blood to drink — Rev 16:3-6

THE FIFTH PLAGUE

Revelation 16:10, 11

10 The fifth angel poured out his bowl on the throne of the beast, and his kingdom was plunged into darkness. Men gnawed their tongues in agony 11 and cursed the God of heaven because of their pains and their sores, but they refused to repent of what they had done.

Darkness — Physical darkness and spiritual darkness

Refused to repent — They refused to obey the messages to the seven churches — Rev 2:5, 16, 21; 3:3, 19

THE SIXTH PLAGUE

Revelation 16:12

12 The sixth angel poured out his bowl on the great river Euphrates, and its water was dried up to prepare the way for the kings from the East.

The sixth plague is a description of the "fall of Babylon" — Rev 14:8; 18:1-5

River Euphrates — In ancient history Darius the Mede dried up the Euphrates River that flowed through the city of Babylon and the city fell in one night. — Dan 5:30, 31

Water — a symbol of people — Rev 17:15

Revelation 17:1, 2, 16-18

One of the seven angels who had the seven bowls came and said to me, "Come, I will show you the punishment of the

Water dried up — people and nations who support the prostitute woman now withdraw their support and the fallen churches crumble.

Seven angels with seven bowls — Rev 15:7

Revelation 17:1, 2, 16-18 (Cont'd)

great prostitute, who sits on many waters. 2 With her the kings of the earth committed adultery and the inhabitants of the earth were intoxicated with the wine of her adulteries."

16 "The beast and the ten horns you saw will hate the prostitute. They will bring her to ruin and leave her naked; they will eat her flesh and burn her with fire. 17 For God has put it into their hearts to accomplish his purpose by agreeing to give the beast their power to rule, until God's words are fulfilled. 18 The woman you saw is the great city that rules over the kings of the earth."

Great prostitute — Symbol of false churches — Rev 17:3-6

Wine of her adulteries — Rev 14:8; 17:4; 18:3

Beast — Nations and people who support the false systems of worship — Rev 17:3, 4; Rev 13:1

Great city — Rev 17:1, 2, 6, 9; 18:10

Revelation 18:9-24

9 "When the kings of the earth who committed adultery with her and shared her luxury see the smoke of her burning, they will weep and mourn over her. 10 Terrified at her torment, they will stand far off and cry:

" 'Woe! Woe, O great city, O Babylon, city of power! In one hour your doom has come!'

Stand far off — nations will withdraw their support

Revelation 18:9-24 (Cont'd)

11 "The merchants of the earth will weep and mourn over her because no one buys their cargoes any more — 12 cargoes of gold, silver, precious stones and pearls; fine linen, purple, silk and scarlet cloth; every sort of citron wood, and articles of every kind made of ivory, costly wood, bronze, iron and marble; 13 cargoes of cinnamon and spice, of incense, myrrh and frankincense, of wine and olive oil, of fine flour and wheat; cattle and sheep; horses and carriages; and bodies and souls of men.

14 "They will say, 'The fruit you longed for is gone from you. All your riches and splendor have vanished, never to be recovered.' 15 The merchants who sold these things and gained their wealth from her will stand far off, terrified at her torment. They will weep and mourn 16 and cry out: 'Woe! Woe, O great city, dressed in fine linen, purple and scarlet, and glittering with gold, precious stones and pearls! 17 In one hour such great wealth has been brought to ruin!'

Stand far off — merchants withdraw their support

Revelation 18:9-24 (Cont'd)

"Every sea captain, and all who travel by ship, the sailors, and all who earn their living from the sea, will stand far off. 18 When they see the smoke of her burning, they will exclaim, 'Was there ever a city like this great city?' 19 They will throw dust on their heads, and with weeping and mourning cry out:

" 'Woe! Woe, O great city, where all who had ships on the sea became rich through her wealth! In one hour she has been brought to ruin!

" '20 Rejoice over her, O heaven! Rejoice, saints and apostles and prophets! God has judged her for the way she treated you.' "

21 Then a mighty angel picked up a boulder the size of a large millstone and threw it into the sea, and said:

"With such violence the great city of Babylon will be thrown down, never to be found again.

"22 The music of harpists and musicians, flute players and trumpeters, will never be heard in you again. No workman of any trade will ever be found in you again. The sound of a

Stand far off — merchant marines withdraw their support
Burning — Rev 14:10, 11

Rejoice saints — Dan 7:27

Large millstone — Dan 2:34, 44, 45

Revelation 18:9-24 (Cont'd)

millstone will never be heard in you again.

"23 The light of a lamp will never shine in you again. The voice of the bridegroom and bride will never be heard in you again. Your merchants were the world's great men. By your magic spell all the nations were led astray.

"24 In her was found the blood of prophets and of the saints, and of all who have been killed on the earth."

Bridegroom — Jn 3:29; Rev 19:7 — Jesus left them never to return
Bride — Rev 21:2, 9, 10

Blood — Rev 17:6

THE SEVENTH PLAGUE

Revelation 16:17-21

17 The seventh angel poured out his bowl into the air, and out of the temple came a loud voice from the throne, saying, "It is done!" 18 Then there came flashes of lightning, rumblings, peals of thunder and a severe earthquake. No earthquake like it has ever occurred since man has been on earth, so tremendous was the quake. 19 The great city split into three parts, and the cities of the

Revelation 16:17-21 (Cont'd)

nations collapsed. God remembered Babylon the Great and gave her the cup filled with the wine of the fury of his wrath. 20 Every island fled away and the mountains could not be found. 21 From the sky huge hailstones of about a hundred pounds each fell upon men. And they cursed God on account of the plague of hail, because the plague was so terrible.

The cup — Rev 17:4; 14:8-10

Mountains — Rev 6:14-16

Hailstones — Rev 6:15, 16

Revelation 19:11-16

11 I saw heaven standing open and there before me was a white horse, whose rider is called Faithful and True. With justice he judges and makes war. 12 His eyes are like blazing fire, and on his head are many crowns. He has a name written on him that no one knows but he himself. 13 He is dressed in a robe dipped in blood, and his name is the Word of God. 14 The armies of heaven were following him, riding on white horses and dressed in fine linen, white and clean. 15 Out of his

White — symbol of purity — Rev 6:1
Horse — Symbol of war and conquering — see note on Rev 6:2
Faithful and True — Jesus Christ — Rev 1:5; 3:14; Jn 18:37
Eyes of blazing fire — Rev 1:14

Robe dipped in blood — Isa 63:1-6
Word of God — Jn 1:1, 14
Jesus comes — 1 Thess 4:16, 17

Revelation 19:11-16 (Cont'd)

mouth comes a sharp sword with which to strike down the nations. "He will rule them with an iron scepter." He treads the winepress of the fury of the wrath of God Almighty. 16 On his robe and on his thigh he has this name written:
KING OF KINGS AND LORD OF LORDS.

Sword — See note on Rev 1:16

Wrath of God — Rev 14:10

King of kings — 1 Tim 6:15, 16 Compare with title on the prostitute woman's forehead — Rev 17:5

Revelation 8:1

When he opened the seventh seal, there was silence in heaven for about half an hour.

The seventh seal suggests that all the heavenly beings are on their way to earth to redeem the saints and take them to heaven.

Revelation 6:14-17

14 The sky receded like a scroll, rolling up, and every mountain and island was removed from its place.
15 Then the kings of the earth, the princes, the generals, the rich, the mighty, and every slave and every free man hid in caves and among the rocks of the mountains. 16 They called to the mountains and the rocks, "Fall on us and hide us from

Revelation 6:14-17 (Cont'd)

the face of him who sits on the throne and from the wrath of the Lamb! 17 For the great day of their wrath has come, and who can stand?"

Sits on the throne — Rev 4:2

Wrath — Rev 14:10, 11

Revelation 14:14-20

14 I looked, and there before me was a white cloud, and seated on the cloud was one "like a son of man" with a crown of gold on his head and a sharp sickle in his hand. 15 Then another angel came out of the temple and called in a loud voice to him who was sitting on the cloud, "Take your sickle and reap, because the time to reap has come, for the harvest of the earth is ripe." 16 So he who was seated on the cloud swung his sickle over the earth, and the earth was harvested.

17 Another angel came out of the temple in heaven, and he too had a sharp sickle. 18 Still another angel, who had charge of the fire, came from the altar and called in a loud voice to him who had the sharp sickle,

Son of man — Mt 25:31-46

Temple — Rev 15:5, 6

Harvest — Mt 13:24-30

Revelation 14:14-20 (Cont'd)

"Take your sharp sickle and gather the clusters of grapes from the earth's vine, because its grapes are ripe." 19 The angel swung his sickle on the earth, gathered its grapes and threw them into the great winepress of God's wrath. 20 They were trampled in the winepress outside the city, and blood flowed out of the press, rising as high as the horses' bridles for a distance of 1,600 stadia.

Revelation 19:17-21

17 And I saw an angel standing in the sun, who cried in a loud voice to all the birds flying in midair, "Come, gather together for the great supper of God, 18 so that you may eat the flesh of kings, generals, and mighty men, of horses and their riders, and the flesh of all people, free and slave, small and great."
19 Then I saw the beast and the kings of the earth and their armies gathered together to make war against the rider on the horse and his army. 20 But the beast was captured, and with

Beast — Rev 13:1
War against rider — Battle of Armageddon — Rev 16:14, 16
Compare Dan 2:44, 45; 7:22, 26, 27; 8:25; 12:1-3
Rider on horse — Rev 19:11-16

Revelation 19:17-21 (Cont'd)

him the false prophet who had performed the miraculous signs on his behalf. With these signs he had deluded those who had received the mark of the beast and worshiped his image. The two of them were thrown alive into the fiery lake of burning sulfur. 21 The rest of them were killed with the sword that came out of the mouth of the rider on the horse, and all the birds gorged themselves on their flesh.

False prophet — Rev 16:13; 17:1-6
Miraculous signs — Rev 13:13

Mark of beast . . . his image — Rev 14:9-11

Sword — Rev 19:15

See p. 94 for "A Study Guide on the Order of Events Close of Probation to the Beginning of the Millennium".

THE LAMB AND THE 144,000

Revelation 14:1-5

Then I looked, and there before me was the Lamb, standing on Mount Zion, and with him 144,000 who had his name and his Father's name written on their foreheads. 2 And I heard a sound from heaven like the roar of rushing waters and like a loud peal of thunder. The sound I heard was like that of harpists playing their harps.

Lamb — Rev 5:6
144,000 — Special group of saints redeemed from earth. This number may be literal or symbolic — Rev 7:1-8
In Rev 7, the 144,000 are being sealed; in this passage they are seen in heaven.
Name written on foreheads — symbol of allegiance to the true God by worshiping Him on the seventh day Sabbath of creation. Rev 7:3

Revelation 14:1-5 (Cont')

3 And they sang a new song before the throne and before the four living creatures and the elders. No one could learn the song except the 144,000 who had been redeemed from the earth. 4 These are those who did not defile themselves with women, for they kept themselves pure. They follow the Lamb wherever he goes. They were purchased from among men and offered as firstfruits to God and the Lamb. 5 No lie was found in their mouths; they are blameless.

In contrast the mark of the beast on the foreheads of those who are lost is acceptance of Sunday worship on the first day of the week. Rev 13:15-17; 14:9-12

Before the throne — Rev 4

VICTORIOUS ON SEA OF GLASS

Revelation 15:2-4

2 And I saw what looked like a sea of glass mixed with fire and, standing beside the sea, those who had been victorious over the beast and his image and over the number of his name. They held harps given them by God 3 and sang the song of Moses the servant of God and the song of the Lamb:

Our attention is now turned to events transpiring in heaven.

Beast and his image — Rev 13:14-17
Number of his name — Rev 13:17, 18

Revelation 15:2-4 (Cont'd)

"Great and marvelous are your deeds, Lord God Almighty. Just and true are your ways, King of the ages.

4 "Who will not fear you, O Lord, and bring glory to your name? For you alone are holy. All nations will come and worship before you, for your righteous acts have been revealed."

THE GREAT MULTITUDE

Revelation 7:9-17

9 After this I looked and there before me was a great multitude that no one could count, from every nation, tribe, people and language, standing before the throne and in front of the Lamb. They were wearing white robes and were holding palm branches in their hands. 10 And they cried out in a loud voice:

"Salvation belongs to our God, who sits on the throne, and to the Lamb."

11 All the angels were standing around the throne and around the elders and the four

Great multitude —
The redeemed from earth

Throne — Rev 4

Revelation 7:9-17 (Cont'd)

living creatures. They fell down on their faces before the throne and worshiped God, 12 saying:

"Amen! Praise and glory and wisdom and thanks and honor and power and strength be to our God for ever and ever. Amen!"

13 Then one of the elders asked me, "These in white robes — who are they, and where did they come from?"

14 I answered, "Sir, you know." And he said, "These are they who have come out of the great tribulation; they have washed their robes and made them white in the blood of the Lamb. 15 Therefore, they are before the throne of God and serve him day and night in his temple; and he who sits on the throne will spread his tent over them.

16 "Never again will they hunger; never again will they thirst. The sun will not beat upon them, nor any scorching heat.

17 "For the Lamb at the center of the throne will be their shepherd; he will lead them to springs of living water. And God will wipe away every tear from their eyes."

Great tribulation — Rev 6:9-11

Sits on the throne — Rev 4:2

Lamb at center of throne — Rev 5:6

A Study Guide On The Order Of Events
Close Of Probation To The Beginning Of The Millennium

Close of Probation → Beginning of Millennium

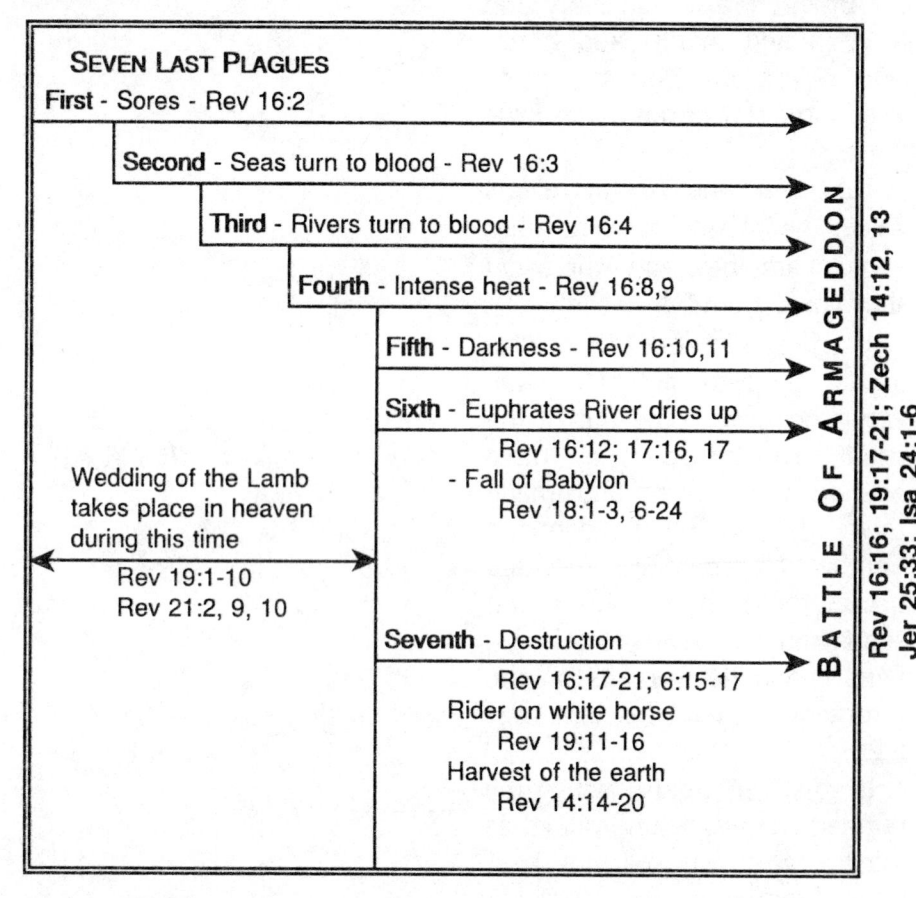

SEVEN LAST PLAGUES
- First - Sores - Rev 16:2
- Second - Seas turn to blood - Rev 16:3
- Third - Rivers turn to blood - Rev 16:4
- Fourth - Intense heat - Rev 16:8,9
- Fifth - Darkness - Rev 16:10,11
- Sixth - Euphrates River dries up
  - Rev 16:12; 17:16, 17
  - Fall of Babylon
  - Rev 18:1-3, 6-24
- Seventh - Destruction
  - Rev 16:17-21; 6:15-17
  - Rider on white horse
  - Rev 19:11-16
  - Harvest of the earth
  - Rev 14:14-20

Wedding of the Lamb takes place in heaven during this time
Rev 19:1-10
Rev 21:2, 9, 10

BATTLE OF ARMAGEDDON — Rev 16:16; 19:17-21; Zech 14:12, 13; Jer 25:33; Isa 24:1-6

For additional reading regarding:
Plagues one to four	GC*	p. 628
Plagues five and seven	GC	p. 635-652 (Chapter 40)
Sixth plague	GC	p. 653-657 (Chapter 41)
Wedding of the Lamb	GC	p. 426-428
Rider on the white horse	GC	p. 640, 641
Harvest of the earth	GC	p. 642

*The Great Controversy (See Appendix)

THE THOUSAND YEARS

Revelation 20:1-6

And I saw an angel coming down out of heaven, having the key to the Abyss and holding in his hand a great chain. 2 He seized the dragon, that ancient serpent, who is the devil, or Satan, and bound him for a thousand years. 3 He threw him into the Abyss, and locked and sealed it over him, to keep him from deceiving the nations anymore until the thousand years were ended. After that, he must be set free for a short time.
4 I saw thrones on which were seated those who had been given authority to judge. And I saw the souls of those who had been beheaded because of their testimony for Jesus and because of the word of God. They had not worshiped the beast or his image and had not received his mark on their foreheads or their hands. They came to life and reigned with Christ a thousand years. 5 (The rest of the dead did not come to life until the thousand years were ended.) This is the first resurrection. 6 Blessed and holy are those who

Abyss — earth

Dragon — Rev 12:9

All the wicked will die when Jesus comes. Rev 19:20, 21
The saved are taken to heaven. I Thes 4:16, 17

Satan has no one to deceive for one thousand years. He is bound to this earth.

Beast or his image — Rev 13:14-17; 15:2

All the redeemed live with Christ in heaven for 1,000 years.
Rest of dead — the wicked who are killed and left on the earth at the second coming of Jesus.

Revelation 20:1-6 (Cont'd)

have part in the first resurrection. The second death has no power over them, but they will be priests of God and of Christ and will reign with him for a thousand years.

HOLY CITY DESCENDS FROM HEAVEN

Revelation 21:1-4

Then I saw a new heaven and a new earth, for the first heaven and the first earth had passed away, and there was no longer any sea. 2 I saw the Holy City, the New Jerusalem, coming down out of heaven from God, prepared as a bride beautifully dressed for her husband. 3 And I heard a loud voice from the throne saying, "Now the dwelling of God is with men, and he will live with them. They will be his people, and God himself will be with them and be their God. 4 He will wipe every tear from their eyes. There will be no more death or mourning or crying or pain, for the old order of things has passed away."

The New Jerusalem, capital city of the universe, is moved to earth. Because of God's great love for man, He now makes this earth the center for the government of the universe and the home of the redeemed.

SATAN'S KINGDOM DESTROYED

Revelation 20:7-15

7 When the thousand years are over, Satan will be released from his prison 8 and will go out to deceive the nations in the four corners of the earth — Gog and Magog — to gather them for battle. In number they are like the sand on the seashore. 9 They marched across the breadth of the earth and surrounded the camp of God's people, the city he loves. But fire came down from heaven and devoured them. 10 And the devil, who deceived them, was thrown into the lake of burning sulfur, where the beast and the false prophet had been thrown. They will be tormented day and night for ever and ever. 11 Then I saw a great white throne and him who was seated on it. Earth and sky fled from his presence, and there was no place for them. 12 And I saw the dead, great and small, standing before the throne, and books were opened. Another book was opened, which is the book of life. The dead were judged according to what they

Deceive the nations — the dead on earth are now raised to life and Satan continues His work of deception.

City he loves — The Holy City (the capital of the universe) is moved from heaven to earth at the end of the 1,000 years. Rev 21:1-4, 9, 10
Burning sulfur — Rev 14:10, 11

For ever and ever — This means that they are completely destroyed forever. The same wording is used in describing the destruction of Sodom and Gomorrah. Jude 7

Dead were judged — Rev 20:4

Revelation 20:7-15 (Cont'd)

had done as recorded in the books. 13 The sea gave up the dead that were in it, and death and Hades gave up the dead that were in them, and each person was judged according to what he had done. 14 Then death and Hades were thrown into the lake of fire. The lake of fire is the second death. 15 If anyone's name was not found written in the book of life, he was thrown into the lake of fire.

Records of the lost are reviewed by the saints during the 1,000 years. After the 1,000 years the wicked are raised to life to receive their final sentence. Rev 20:3, 5, 7

Death and Hades — See note on Rev 6:8

All of the wicked are thrown into the lake of fire.

THE NEW JERUSALEM

Revelation 21:9-27

9 One of the seven angels who had the seven bowls full of the seven last plagues came and said to me, "Come, I will show you the bride, the wife of the Lamb." 10 And he carried me away in the Spirit to a mountain great and high, and showed me the Holy City, Jerusalem, coming down out of heaven from God. 11 It shone with the glory of God, and its brilliance was like that of a very precious jewel, like a jasper, clear as crystal. 12 It had a great, high wall with

See Rev 21:2

Revelation 21:9-27 (Cont'd)

twelve gates, and with twelve angels at the gates. On the gates were written the names of the twelve tribes of Israel. 13 There were three gates on the east, three on the north, three on the south and three on the west. 14 The wall of the city had twelve foundations, and on them were the names of the twelve apostles of the Lamb.

15 The angel who talked with me had a measuring rod of gold to measure the city, its gates and its walls. 16 The city was laid out like a square, as long as it was wide. He measured the city with the rod and found it to be 12,000 stadia in length, and as wide and high as it is long. 17 He measured its wall and it was 144 cubits thick, by man's measurement, which the angel was using. 18 The wall was made of jasper, and the city of pure gold, as pure as glass. 19 The foundations of the city walls were decorated with every kind of precious stone. The first foundation was jasper, the second sapphire, the third chalcedony, the fourth emerald, 20 the fifth sardonyx, the sixth carnelian, the seventh chrysolite,

Revelation 21:9-27 (Cont'd)

the eighth beryl, the ninth topaz, the tenth chrysoprase, the eleventh jacinth, and the twelfth amethyst. 21 The twelve gates were twelve pearls, each gate made of a single pearl. The great street of the city was of pure gold, like transparent glass.

22 I did not see a temple in the city, because the Lord God Almighty and the Lamb are its temple. 23 The city does not need the sun or the moon to shine on it, for the glory of God gives it light, and the Lamb is its lamp. 24 The nations will walk by its light, and the kings of the earth will bring their splendor into it. 25 On no day will its gates ever be shut, for there will be no night there. 26 The glory and honor of the nations will be brought into it. 27 Nothing impure will ever enter it, nor will anyone who does what is shameful or deceitful, but only those whose names are written in the Lamb's book of life.

THE RIVER OF LIFE

Revelation 22:1-6

Then the angel showed me the river of the water of life, as clear as crystal, flowing from the throne of God and of the Lamb 2 down the middle of the great street of the city. On each side of the river stood the tree of life, bearing twelve crops of fruit, yielding its fruit every month. And the leaves of the tree are for the healing of the nations. 3 No longer will there be any curse. The throne of God and of the Lamb will be in the city, and his servants will serve him. 4 They will see his face, and his name will be on their foreheads. 5 There will be no more night. They will not need the light of a lamp or the light of the sun, for the Lord God will give them light. And they will reign for ever and ever.

6 The angel said to me, "These words are trustworthy and true. The Lord, the God of the spirits of the prophets, sent his angel to show his servants the things that must soon take place."

Things that must soon take place. — Rev 1:1

The grace of the Lord Jesus be with His people. Rev 22:21

APPENDIX

GENERAL NOTES

Page 38. THE THRONE IN HEAVEN, CHRIST BEGINS MINISTRY IN HEAVEN. For a more detailed description see Ellen G. White, <u>The Desire of Ages</u>, pp. 832-835. Available at your local Christian book store or Pacific Press Publishing Association, Nampa, Idaho 83651.

Pages 43, 66 THE FOUR SEALS. For more information see Ellen G. White, <u>The Great Controversy Between Christ and Satan</u>, pp. 39-60. Available at your local Christian book store or Pacific Press Publishing Association, Nampa, Idaho 83651.

FILTH OF HER ADULTERIES
Rev 17:4

	False Teachings	Word of God
1.	Pope visible head of universal church	Christ head of Church Col 1:18; Eph 5:23
2.	Pope has authority over all bishops and pastors	Christ is the authority John 17:1, 2
3.	Pope assumes title of deity "Lord God the Pope"	Only one God Ex 20:3; I Tim 1:17
4.	Pope declared "infallible"	All have sinned Rom 5:12
5.	All to give Pope homage or worship	Worship God only Ex 20:4, 5; Lk 4:8
6.	Prohibited circulation of Bible	All Scripture profitable 2 Tim 3:16; Ps 119; Mt 28:19, 20
7.	Adoration of images	Image worship prohibited Ex 20:4, 5
8.	Made Sunday a day of worship in place of the seventh day Sabbath	Seventh day sanctified Gen 2:2, 3; Ex 20:8-11
9.	Pope claims to be Christ's earthly mediator	Jesus is only Mediator Act 4:12; I Tim 2:5
10.	Church claims it never erred nor would err	All have sinned Rom 3:23; I Jn 1:10
11.	Man is immortal	God alone is immortal I Tim 6:15, 16

Filth of her Adulteries (Cont'd)

	False Teachings	**Word of God**
12.	Man is conscious in death	Dead know nothing Ps 146:4; Ec 9:5, 6, 10
13.	Invocation of saints	Present requests to God Phil 4:6
14.	Adoration of Mary	Worship God only Ex 20:3-6; Matt 4:10
15.	Eternal torment	First earth destroyed; all things new Rev 21:1, 5
16.	Purgatory	Dead have no life Ps 146:4; Ec 9:5, 6, 10
17.	Doctrine of indulgences	Justified freely by grace Rom 3:23, 24
18.	Pay money to free themselves from sin	Forgiveness is through Christ Lk 5:21-24
19.	Sacrifice of the mass	The Lord's Supper Lk 22:17-20; I Cor 11:23-26
20.	The Inquisition	Persecution by beast power Dan 7:21; Rev 13:7
21.	Celibacy of priests and nuns	Be fruitful and increase Gen 1:28
22.	Confession to priests	Confess to God Rom 14:11, 12; I Jn 1:9
23.	Presumed to change God's law	Dan 7:25 - see next page

TEN COMMANDMENTS

Exodus 20:3-17 (NIV) As Written by the Finger of God

I

3 "You shall have no other gods before me.

II

4 "You shall not make for yourself an idol in the form of anything in heaven above or on the earth beneath or in the waters below. 5 You shall not bow down to them or worship them; for I, the Lord your God, am a jealous God, punishing the children for the sin of the fathers to the third and fourth generation of those who hate me, 6 but showing love to a thousand generations of those who love me and keep my commandments.

III

7 "You shall not misuse the name of the Lord your God, for the Lord will not hold anyone guiltless who misuses his name.

TEN COMMANDMENTS

As Abbreviated in Vernacular Roman Catholic Catechism

I

I am the Lord thy God. Thou shalt not have strange gods before Me.

(Deleted)

II

Thou shalt not take the name of the Lord thy God in vain.

IV

8 "Remember the Sabbath day by keeping it holy. 9 Six days you shall labor and do all your work, 10 but the seventh day is a Sabbath to the Lord your God. On it you shall not do any work, neither you, nor your son or daughter, nor your manservant or maidservant, nor your animals, nor the alien within your gates. 11 For in six days the Lord made the heavens and the earth, the sea, and all that is in them, but he rested on the seventh day. Therefore the Lord blessed the Sabbath day and made it holy.

V

12 "Honor your father and your mother, so that you may live long in the land the Lord your God is giving you.

VI

13 "You shall not murder.

VII

14 "You shall not commit adultery.

III

Remember thou keep holy the Sabbath day.

IV

Honor thy father and thy mother.

V

Thou shalt not kill.

VI

Thou shalt not commit adultery.

VIII

15 "You shall not steal.

IX

16 "You shall not give false testimony against your neighbor.

X

17 "You shall not covet your neighbor's house. You shall not covet your neighbor's wife, or his manservant or maidservant, his ox or donkey, or anything that belongs to your neighbor."

VII

Thou shalt not steal.

VIII

Thou shalt not bear false witness against thy neighbor.

IX

Thou shalt not covet thy neighbor's wife.

X

Thou shalt not covet thy neighbor's goods.

NOTE: Compare the changes between the Ten Commandments written by God and the Ten Commandments written by those that "try to change the set times and the laws." Dan 7:25.

1. The second is omitted.
2. The fourth is abbreviated and is listed as the third.
3. The tenth is divided into two commandments (numbers nine and ten) and is also abbreviated.

The Altar of Burnt Offerings

The Altar of Burnt Offerings was the part of the sanctuary service that brought the individual worshiper the closest to the process of salvation. Two things every sinner must do to be forgiven his sins: he must come to the sanctuary bringing an animal for sacrifice (the size of the sacrifice depended upon his financial status, if he were wealthy, it might be a heifer or a lamb; if he were poor, it could be a turtledove or even a handful of flour) and the sinner must lay his hands on the head of the animal sacrifice and confess his sins. Then, with his own hands, he killed the sacrificial animal.

Most of the sin-offering ritual was attended to by the priests but the essence of the sin-offering was that the sinner, by confessing his sins over the lamb, in type and shadow transferred them to the lamb. The life of the lamb was then taken instead of the life of the sinner, typifying the death of the Lamb of God who would offer His life for the sins of the world.

Table of Shewbread

The Table of Shewbread was on the north side of the first apartment of the sanctuary. The table was two cubits long, a cubit and a half wide and a cubit and a half high. As with most of the sanctuary furniture, it was made of acacia wood overlaid with pure gold and had an ornamental edging of pure gold around the top. All of the ritual concerning the Table of Shewbread took place on the Sabbath day. Every Sabbath day the Levites made twelve loaves or cakes of unleavened bread. These cakes were placed on the table hot each Sabbath day, arranged in two piles, six to a pile, with pure frankincense on each pile. This bread, called "the bread of the presence" in some translations, lay on the table the entire week. Each week the bread was removed and eaten by the priests, and fresh hot bread was again placed on the table. The bread represented the Word of God--to be assimilated and become a part of our daily lives.

The Golden Candlestick

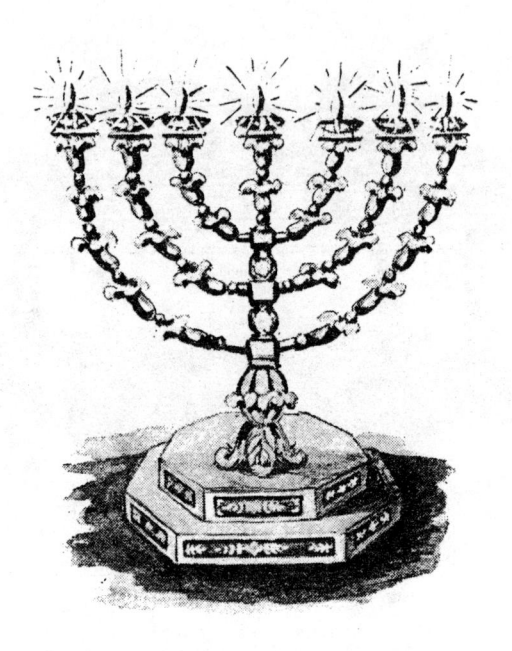

The golden candlestick with its seven golden lamps was on the south side of the first apartment of the sanctuary. It was made of gold beaten into shape by the hammer of the master craftsmen. It took many hard and skillful blows to form the delicate flowers and bowls; however, the candlestick must be made after the heavenly model to teach heavenly lessons to mankind.

The number seven in the Bible denotes a complete number, and the candlestick with its seven bowls for lamps represented the church of God through the ages, holding up the light of truth in the midst of moral darkness.

Altar of Incense

The golden Altar of Incense stood before the veil in the first apartment of the sanctuary. It was one cubit square and two cubits high, and had a horn on each corner. It was made of acacia wood all overlaid with pure gold and had an ornamental edging of pure gold around the top, and just under the edging were rings of gold for the carrying staves.

Within the crown of gold encircling the top of the altar, holy fire was kept constantly burning from which rose the fragrant smoke that represented the prayers of the people ascending to heaven.

The incense, composed of an equal weight of four fragrant gums and resins, was prepared by divine direction, and any person making it for private use was to be cut off from among the people.

Ark of the Covenant

The ark was the central figure of the entire sanctuary. The broken law contained in the ark was the only reason for all the sacrificial services, both typical and antitypical. As with the other sanctuary furniture, explicit instructions were given as to size and design. The ark, however, was overlaid with gold both inside and outside. The cover of the ark was called the mercy seat and was of pure gold. On the ends of the mercy seat were cherubim of beaten gold, with their wings outstretched covering the ark, and their faces looking reverently toward the law of God contained therein.

God communed with His people from the cloud of glory which rested above the mercy seat between the cherubim. These golden cherubim with outstretched wings were a representation of the covering cherubim that surround the throne of God in heaven.